Joy Baker

Trailblazer for home-based education and personalised learning

by Chris Shute

Educational Heretics Press

Published 2008 by Educational Heretics Press
113 Arundel Drive, Bramcote, Nottingham NG9 3FQ

Copyright © 2008 Educational Heretics Press

British Cataloguing in Publication Data

Shute, Chris
    Joy Baker:
    trailblazer for home-based education and
    personalised learning
    1.Baker, Joy 2. Home schooling
    1. Title
    371'.042'092

ISBN   978-1-900219-35-8

This book is sold subject to the condition that it shall not, by way of trade or otherwise, be lent, re-sold, hired out, or otherwise circulated without the publisher's prior consent in any form of binding or cover other than that in which it is published and without a similar condition being imposed on the subsequent purchasers.

Design and production: Educational Heretics Press

Cover design by Educational Heretics Press

Printed by Mastaprint Plus, Sandiacre, Nottingham NG10 5AH

Contents

Introduction		1
Chapter 1	Joy Baker and Education Otherwise Than At School	9
Chapter 2	Battle Is Joined	17
Chapter 3	Joy's Alternative Philosophy of Learning	25
Chapter 4	A Mad World, My Masters	33
Chapter 5	Quis Custodiet? (Who Will Guard The Guards?)	49
Chapter 6	The Authorities Counterattack	79
Chapter 7	Back in Court	83
Chapter 8	Up the Down Escalator	95
Chapter 9	The Last Stretch	103
Chapter 10	Conclusion and Postscipt	113

Introduction

My training college had a fine library. It was housed in the octagonal building which had served as the Practice School in the early days of formal school teaching. The room was divided into four large bays, where it was not difficult to imagine classes of more or less ragged children being piloted through the rocks and sand-banks of long division, grammar and elementary geography by four young men, standing back to back and struggling to be heard as they drove their lessons into their pupils' heads.

Their work, and the system it was designed to serve were a graphic portrayal of nineteenth century priorities. It was inexpensive, economical in terms of manpower, and easily supervised. It expressed the conviction, endemic at the time, that life was a grim, rather joyless affair if you had the misfortune to be born outside the ranks of the privileged.

We no longer expect teachers to work in what amounts to a bullring. We have accepted that education needs at least a modicum of privacy if it is to 'work'. Schools have been built to look a little less like factories, and the ratio between the numbers of pupils and teachers has become more reasonable than the 90:1 which was common in the nineteenth century.

Yet schools have not yet become places where every honest person would be willing to send their children. More and more families are looking at their children and then at the schools to which they have to send them and realising that for them, at least, the equation school equals education does not make sense.

In many cases they have been able to observe their children's discovery of life in all its amazing variety and fullness and have realised that most of what the youngsters have learned came to them without the mediation of teachers, prepared lessons and the rag-bag curriculum so dear to school administrators. This perception often moves them to stop sending their children to school, or even to refuse to enrol them there in the first place.

The Education Act of 1944, as well as its subsequent amendments, allows children to be educated 'by attendance at school or otherwise'. It is possible that this apparently broad-minded provision was added to the Act mainly to meet the needs of well-off people who could afford to pay for private tutors. Certainly the generality of school authorities did not expect to have to deal with 'ordinary' parents who refused to send their children to state schools.

In the culture of the time, any parents who fell outside the charmed circle of the specially privileged and who hesitated to entrust their children to a school were considered to be either feckless or socially deviant and malicious. In either case the remedy was simple, and redolent of simpler-minded times: threaten them with the courts, and if that did not scare them into compliance, fine them, imprison them, and take their children into care for their own good.

It is possible to imagine situations in which at least part of that approach could, in the long run, help to rescue a genuinely deprived child from a corrosive and depressing family environment. As a foster-carer myself I have seen families whose children were silently crying out to be removed and given the peace and attention they needed in order to become happy and positive adults. Yet in no case have I seen parents whose refusal to send their children to school was crushing their spirit and driving them into criminal behaviour and fugues. It was always lack of love and deep emotional neglect which had that effect.

That is why the story of Joy Baker attracts me. I vaguely remember reading about her stand against compulsory schooling when I was a schoolboy myself, but it was only after I retired from teaching and began to be interested in the development of home-based education that I saw clearly how essentially heroic she was. I have spoken to local authority officials on behalf of home-based educating parents and met with a variety of responses, from suspicion and even disdain to positive approval.

In Joy Baker's time, no-one had thought seriously about whether schools could meet the needs of all children. Like many other aspects of life just after the war, going to school was just one of the things which people did because they had reached a certain age or a certain position in life. Like criminals, poor people who could not pay their bills, young men of military age and many unskilled workers, children were thought of as 'needing' a more or less harsh and unresponsive environment in which they would experience and become inured to the hard knocks which life would undoubtedly deal out to them. Governments were not willing to let the idealism which drove their political programmes, leak out of their manifestos and into the lives of ordinary citizens. Consequently, they spoke much about all the new opportunities which the 1944 Education Act would offer to children, but did absolutely nothing to make going to school less of an ordeal for individual children.

Joy Baker believed that she could do a better job of educating her children than the state could, in spite of its good intentions. She not only loved her children - most parents do that - but she also liked them and enjoyed their company. She foresaw that if she sent them to school not only would they be corrupted in many subtle ways, but that she would not be able to respond to their unique patterns of intellectual growth, answering their questions and making possible their discovery of the world in which we live.

She was certainly unusual, particularly in her belief that education was part of the panoply of responsibilities which belong to parents, and only by default to other people, such as teachers and school administrators. Her generation was used to the idea that the state stood in the same relationship to individual citizens as a father did to his children. By refusing to send her children to school she was challenging not only the letter of the law but also one of the most deeply rooted and durable presuppositions which determine our culture. She was refusing to be a compliant cog in society's machine, and that society responded to her 'rebellion' with all the anger and disproportionate vehemence which we have become used to seeing whenever one person refuses to bow to the state's authority.

She was, without knowing it, a pioneer of education out of school. She did not think of herself as starting a movement or creating a new education system. As I read her book, *Children in Chancery*, I found myself in the presence of a true individualist. She was not concerned with anyone else's children, or with any wider implications her ideas might have. She was moved by the single thought that she, who had brought her children into the world, knew what they needed and felt absolutely entitled to give it to them in whatever way seemed right to her.

She ran into trouble with the education authorities because they could not see in her discursive, child-centred methods anything which they could recognise as analogous to what they were doing in schools. I share her bafflement at their bizarre conviction that in education, unlike any other field of human activity, the process is supremely important, whilst the results it procures have relatively minor significance.

In our culture it is more important that children attend school than that it do them any good. Even if they reject schooling with every fibre of their being, our educational establishment would rather see them forced to go to a place which they hate, to do work which fills them with resentment than find some other interesting and enjoyable activity for them to do. From time to time our society even goes to the morally indefensible extreme of putting parents in jail when they fail to make their children go to school, with consequences which cannot easily be estimated but which it is certain have no positive side to them.

There is, of course, no certain way of determining exactly why a liberal, democratic society such as we were even in Joy Baker's day would devote such enormous effort to accomplishing so manifestly wrong-headed an aim as that of putting all children through a process which left a proportion of them intellectually disabled. Perhaps it stems from the ancient idea that if we make life too pleasant and untroubled for our children they will grow up without the military virtues of endurance and self-denial. Certainly it suggests an ignorance of the way children and young people think and learn which would be devastating if it were applied to medicine and the working of their physical body.

I would suggest that we are beginning to pay the price of our folly. Most of our young people spend 11 years at state schools. and emerge with some sort of academic certificate. Some of them go on to have normal careers, but a worrying minority, which seems to be growing in size, use drugs, commit various crimes and in rare, but intensely disturbing cases, arm themselves with knives and even handguns and go out to avenge trivial slights with attacks which sometimes lead to death. If we believe that what we expose our children to affects, and even determines their behaviour, surely we should be asking ourselves whether any of the experiences which we force on our children by law are causing some of them to become vicious, and even homicidal.

I would conclude that if schooling is compulsory for most children, it has no business ending up in failure.

8 Chris Shute

Chapter one

Joy Baker and Education Otherwise than at School

Joy Baker's children were born just after the Second World War. Britain was emerging from the straitjacket of wartime necessity. People were used to doing as authority told them, because war does not defer to individual tastes and preferences. It sweeps them aside and puts in their place grim simplicities such as DORA (Defence of the Realm Act), conscription and rationing.

Education was no exception to this culture of constraint and forced obedience. Even when the war was over it seemed natural to expect parents to see sending their children to school as a reasonable part of a pattern of life which would later include National Service, and would always expect them to submit to social constraints founded on a class system many centuries old.

Joy Baker liked her children very much. She loved them as well, but unlike many parents, who also love their children, and want the best for them, she did not look forward to the time when she could hand them over, body and soul to someone else for their education. Her own experience of schooling which had left her convinced that the sort of education she had suffered could only harm her children, and she acted on that conviction.

She was young, only 21 years old, when her first child was born. She had vivid memories of her years in school, which she described as *"eight years of hell"*, and she had emerged from them with a *"fixed determination that I would never condemn my own children to a similar waste of the happiest years of their life."*

It is, perhaps, difficult for people such as us, who live in comfort and relative tranquillity, to share the feelings of ordinary British workers and housewives, and particularly minor officials, who had just emerged from nearly six years of terror and destruction, dealt out even-handedly to military and civilian alike. To suggest that children were sensitive, more easily hurt and frustrated than adults, and in need of special care and consideration might well have seemed the height of absurdity to a generation which had been brought up by Victorians and had lived through a war in which millions of children had been destroyed by bombing or murdered in pursuit of state policy.

Joy Baker's insistence on her right to educate her children at home certainly struck the authorities at the time as simply unnecessary. All children went to school because it 'did them good' and taught them their proper place in the scheme of things. If they found parts of the experience hard to bear, well, life was like that, and they might as well learn the lesson when they were young.

At an even more basic level, schooling was the law. Parliament had added to the list of obligations which weighed on a citizen the duty to send any children he or she might have to a school. To cover the tiny proportion of families, well-off and aristocratic, who would continue to pay tutors to educate their children, the new law required everyone to see that their children received education 'by attendance at school or otherwise'. No-one, it may be surmised, expected or intended that this provision would be used to keep ordinary children out of school. Local authorities worked on the principle that any non-aristocratic parents who did not send their young to the local school were simply lawbreakers who would have to be pursued, with a certain amount of regret, but rigorously through the sordid charade of the magistrates court, in the same way as drunks, petty thieves and disturbers of the peace.

In her book *Children in Chancery*, Joy Baker describes her encounters with local authority officials. They were marked by what looks like mutual incomprehension, but which I would argue was more like a conflict between two theologies, which could not be reconciled because each believed implicitly that their own doctrine was the only tenable set of beliefs.

When any belief-system becomes settled in the collective mind of a group of people it tends to lose any relativistic aspects it might have had. Before very long adherence to it becomes the mark of a loyal member of that community. To challenge it is then to be an enemy of everything that community stands for. It no longer matters how valid or reasonable the contrary position may be, it is simply and starkly false. Joy Baker became a heretic, and consequently a number of men and women who would never have agreed in principle with cruelty to children felt compelled to drag hers through the courts, threaten them and even abduct them from the security of their home late at night.

Two approaches to education clashed over a period of several years. During her court appearances Joy Baker explained in detail how she was educating her children. She was articulate, graphic in her description of a process which could not justly be described as harmful to her children, and passionate in her defence of her right as a parent to be the main influence in her children's lives.

The authorities wearily repeated their insistence that the law required her to send her children to school. They could not allow her to establish any of her arguments, not because they were not valid, but because they expressed a view of the world in which the officials themselves, and the framework of thought which they had grown up with and were now paid to administer, had no place.

Of course, the usual courtesies were observed. The education authorities wrote to Joy asking her what she intended to do about her children's education, and she wrote back endless letters in which she told them clearly that she would do everything which needed to be done to give her children the knowledge and skill that they needed. The authorities were not satisfied, and demanded the right to come to her house and see what she was doing with the children. On the face of it this may have seemed like a reasonable request. After all, the authorities saw themselves

A New Education Act

as having a duty to ensure that children in their area were properly educated. One might reasonably ask how they were to fulfil that duty if they could not see those children while they were being educated.

Joy Baker's reply took the form of a challenge:

> "I am their parent, and I say that they are adequately educated. My word is sufficient proof in itself, and you need only accept it and leave me alone to finish the work I have started."

This is, perhaps, the central dilemma which haunts all lawmakers in the advanced culture to which western society lays claim. We have, through many centuries of struggle and debate, finally reached a point where we pass laws for the benefit of everybody. We no longer have 'the rich man in his castle, the poor man at his gate', and we no longer accept that 'God made them high and lowly and ordered their estate.' We have a National Health Service which treats everyone free at the point of need. We give rights to all our citizens without distinction, and we assume that our laws apply equally to every citizen.

In return, we expect every citizen to appreciate the services we offer them, and to do whatever needs to be done in order to distribute our national resources fairly. This all seems reasonable. Yet it rides roughshod over at least one fundamental democratic principle - that each individual is entitled to dissent from the State's interpretation of his or her rights, and to argue for a different approach to them.

This may mean that the dissenter rejects what seems to a professional observer like good sense. As our life has become more organised and complex we have become used to the idea that certain people, known as professionals, have mastered difficult skills, like medicine, architecture and the law, and that when the need arises to solve problems in these fields we must turn to these people and submit unquestioningly to their opinion. In return for their work, they generally command high salaries or fees, and they receive a measure of respect which is not given to others whose work seems to be based less on intellectual prowess and more on skill in practicalities such as craftsmanship.

One baneful consequence of this state of affairs is that anyone whose work calls for a certain measure of intelligence will tend to want professional status, with all the unchallengeable mystification which goes with it. Teachers have struggled for more than a century to join the ranks of the professionals, and have to a large extent succeeded.

Teachers in state schools began as apprentices, selected from among the brighter pupils and allowed to learn their trade by watching their head teacher and following his or her direction. They did not see themselves as members of a profession, and were not paid more than the average worker's wages. A hundred years later teachers start their first job in possession of a degree in education, a theoretical knowledge of pedagogy gained by three or four years of study, and a conviction that theirs is a complex, at least semi-scientific, network of skills which no untrained person could be expected to be able to practise.

Joy Baker challenged the idea that teaching is a valuable, professional business which automatically benefits all children simply by their being submitted to it. By doing so she exposed logical falsity of the idea as well as the lack within compulsory schooling of the humanistic spirit which so many of us assume to be its *raison d'etre*.

She felt herself to have been the victim of a barren and dispiriting education. She describes it in terms which forcibly contradict the saying that 'schooldays are the happiest days of your life'.

> *"All the fragile world of my childhood, with its idyllic background of an old-fashioned country garden, peopled for me with animals and birds and flowers and the endless fabric of my imagination, was suddenly exposed to what seemed to me a howling mob of strangers; and my daydreams, which were deeply rooted and very precious to me, seemed about as secure as the head of a French aristocrat on the way to the guillotine. Throughout every moment of my eight years of school I felt myself to be under attack; surrounded by an unreal world of potential enemies and present hostility. To assume that any child could receive proper education under such circumstances was patently absurd; and its main effect was in fact to leave me predisposed to be suspicious and defensive towards all interference by an artificial authority."*

It is important to record her own experience of schooling because it reveals starkly the reasons why she was so determined to preserve her own children from such interference with their happiness and harmonious growth. In our supposedly advanced and technological western culture we have grown used to the proposition that children need stress and imposed training. Joy's own parents, she records, had sent her to school because they felt like so many other people, without really knowing why, that children ought to go to school.

Ironically, they later admitted to her that they would have done better to educate her at home, and, even more ironically, they would have been able to do so without official interference since the constraints against which she found herself battling when she tried to educate her children out of school came into being only with the 1944 Education Act.

Chapter two

Battle Is Joined

Joy Baker's first encounter with the new realities of education came about in 1952, when her eldest children, David and Robin, were aged six and five. An Education Welfare Officer came to visit her. She received him without enthusiasm, and gave him very little information. She regarded his visit as a piece of officiousness with no purpose beyond the old-fashioned Wag Man's need to be seen around the neighbourhood trying to drag reluctant pupils into school. Since she had no intention of putting her boys into a traditional classroom she assumed that she would see no more of the authorities. She still nourished the belief, which the 1944 Act had appeared to suppress, that though an English parent was expected to educate his or her children, the way they set about doing it was their business, and no-one else's.

In July 1952 the Director of Education for Bedfordshire wrote her the first of a veritable library of letters. He acknowledged her right to educate her children otherwise than in school, and then, in a single sentence, abolished it:

"To give effect to the law of education it is essential that efficient full-time education be provided, and the responsibility for its provision rests upon the parent. I must therefore request that a copy of the timetable and scheme of work which your sons will

follow, together with the qualifications of the tutor, be submitted for the approval of the Local Education Authority."

Joy Baker found this supposedly reasonable request absurd. To her way of thinking, unless parents were demonstrably shiftless and irresponsible, the form which education was to take would emerge from those parents' relationship with their children, and could no more be planned in advance than tomorrow's weather. The director's request for details of 'the timetable and the schemes of work' which she proposed to use seemed to her absolutely alien to the idea of education which she had derived from her own childhood, when her parents had educated her out of school for two years, before sending her to school for the first time. As for the 'qualifications of the tutor', her parents were 'unqualified', but had taught her to read and write successfully.

She expressed her convictions to the director, who replied with what must have seemed to him like sweet reasonableness, but what to Joy sounded much more like impertinence. A dialogue of the deaf began, in which the director continued to insist on his right to 'authorise' Joy's concept of education, and she repeated tirelessly that she was competent to educate her children, and intended to do so without reference to him.

Meanwhile her children continued to grow and flourish. They had a large, old-fashioned garden in which to play, adjoining a field, which Joy owned, but had let to a farmer to graze his cattle in. There were four Jersey cows, a mare in foal and several ponies. The children played with the cows, even sitting on their backs sometimes, and the farmer gave them rides on his ponies. They saw the foal being born, and thus were introduced naturally to one of the greatest of life's mysteries. Indoors, the children had a playroom filled with toys and what Joy and they called 'things', odd, unrelated pieces of wood, metal, broken toys and bits of furniture, which they used to develop their imagination and their creative powers.

It was an environment in which, I suspect, any serious educator, from Jean-Jacques Rousseau onwards, would have given their eye-teeth to bring up a child. One of the first principles of education which was doled out to me in college was that children learn best when they are at ease and their interest is thoroughly engaged. Joy's house would certainly have provided them with both ease and interest, particularly as, unlike an ordinary teacher, she had the wisdom to keep out of their play and not try to direct it.

"I never prompted or interfered with their play;" she wrote, *"preferring to watch their minds expanding, like opening buds, rather than trying to pull the petals out before they were ready to flower."* (P18)

She began to teach her son, David, to read. Unconstrained by the imperatives of the classroom, to make progress at every lesson, she was able to respond sensitively to his initial unreadiness to grasp the technical challenge of reading. She obtained:

"various school reading books for the purpose, but I soon found that the process was useless; he made no real progress, often being unable to remember words he had read five minutes before, and was soon distressed and bored. I found too that the words and phrases used in these learning to read books , being chosen to group together words with the same sounds, bore no relation to ordinary speech, and this caused the children nothing but confusion until I explained what the right word really was. In the end I gave the children the books to play with, and got instead the Pooh books by A. A. Milne and Kenneth Grahame's The Wind in the Willows, which I read to them every night; and I abandoned reading lessons altogether. David then frequently came to me wanting to know the meaning of a word he had picked out in one of the books, and I found that these words he remembered and understood."

She discovered almost at once what John Holt and others in the field of child-centred education only realised after many years of observation - that children learn a great many things without being taught them, simply by being around grown-ups who do things. Holt records a visit he made to a Danish school where the reading teacher had progressively abandoned the systematic teaching of reading and replaced it with a policy which consisted simply of allowing children to see and use books and giving them the right to ask any question they wished to, at any time. Also, whenever a child wanted to test his or her knowledge of reading they needed to do no more than come to the teacher with a book and read to him as long as they felt was right. He found that the average child took about 30 hours to master reading.

The traditional patterns of school-teaching have imposed on all educational thinking a pre-supposition that learning has to be a process of moving from the 'easy' to the 'difficult', whatever that may mean in relation to a given discipline. For instance, all foreign language courses begin with lessons in which the main verbs are in the present tense: the pen of my aunt **is** always on the bureau of my uncle. Yet even a brief consideration of the language people actually need to know when they go abroad will reveal that the past and the future tenses are far more useful. Beyond mentioning where one lives and what one does for a living, the present tense has precious little application in the context of a holiday in a foreign country. Tourists mainly want to talk about what they will do tomorrow, and what has happened to their luggage. Good language teaching should begin with verbs in the past and future tenses, and with words which are relevant to a normal person's needs, instead of the relentlessly twee and middle-class stuff so often presented to young learners.

The same applies to reading, as Joy Baker discovered. Other subjects may need to be presented in a fixed order, but anything like language, which is a mode of self-expression and capable of being used for any purpose, should not be treated as a set of discrete facts, to be memorised and arranged. The learner should be free to encounter words in as wide a variety of contexts as he or she will in real life. There are no 'easy' and 'difficult' words, only words which the reader wants to read and those which he does not.

In this connection I remember meeting Kaye Webb, the managing editor of Puffin Books, at one time the main publisher of books for children. She insisted that all her authors introduce into their stories words which they knew ordinary children would not know. Her approach to reading came from her understanding that when children have perceived the pleasure and interest which can come to them from reading, they do not need to be seduced into it by any artificial means, such as the pruning of unfamiliar words, or the use of a graded and cumulative vocabulary. Children can learn and use any words in their language as long as they are interesting and in context.

As it happened, Joy Baker's boys, David and Robin, did not begin to read at precisely the point in their development when the school system expects children to start to read. This did not worry her, and she did not make the mistake of thinking of them as 'backward' and pressuring them to do what they were not yet ready to do. Instead:

> *"David and Robin continued to grow up and develop in their own way; they investigated words and numbers in their own time, and drew letters and figures for amusement on rainy days; they asked endless questions about everything they thought of, and played with great energy and enthusiasm. None of this, apparently, met with the approval of the education authorities."*

Battle is Joined 23

The dialogue of the deaf went on. Joy asserted her right to educate her children as she saw fit: the authorities ground out letter after letter in which they insisted that she must allow them to inspect her 'work' and approve of it, if they felt able to. The Clerk of the Council set out the bureaucrats' position:

> *"In reply to your letter of the 28th April I know that you are satisfied that your sons are being properly educated but the point is that the County Council must be satisfied. When they know the facts they might well share your view but until they know how your sons are being educated they are unable to form their own opinion. Since you decline to give this information it does not seem that there is much point in continuing this correspondence."*

As we look back from the relative safety of the twenty-first century, when many local authorities accept home-based education, and do not criticise parents for the unschool-likeness of their provisions, it is easy to feel indignant at the barren operation of petty power, which solved its problem with Joy by serving her with school attendance orders for David and Robin. They were to attend the village school, and that, it was hoped, would be the end of the matter.

Joy tore the orders into small pieces and returned them to the education authority. Small gestures often reveal large emotions. Clearly she no longer thought of herself as a mere citizen, defending her established rights against a clumsy but ultimately reasonable authority. She felt more like a female animal at bay, protecting her young against all comers. She intended her persecutors to know that, in her eyes at least, they and the system they represented could offer her nothing with which she felt any need to comply.

This cannot have been easy for her to do. She lived at a time when deference was more or less universal, and she came from a class which assumed that the law was there to be obeyed, especially since its main function was defend worthy, conforming people like her from their natural enemies, the lawless folk who lived chaotic lives on the margins of society. I cannot account for the precise manner in which she expressed her dissent, but I suspect that the primeval instinct of a mother to protect her young played a major part in her decision to throw down the gauntlet to the authorities.

The authorities replied with a summons. Joy felt she could not take time out from her busy daily schedule to go to the court, and she pleaded not guilty by letter, emphasising that she did not intend to send her children to school because they were receiving 'efficient and suitable education at home'. She was fined £1 for each child, but having pleaded not guilty she was able to appeal against the decision.

Chapter three

Joy's Alternative Philosophy of Learning

The court case coincided with Joy's decision to move from her home at Apsley Guise, and indeed to leave Bedfordshire entirely. In September 1953 she moved to Haddenham, near Aylesbury, and shortly after that to St. Leonards in Buckinghamshire. Perhaps she saw moving house as a means of diverting attention from herself, at least for a short time. In fact it won her a respite of some six months.

In February 1954 the local authority seems to have sent a lady called Mrs Davies to visit Joy's new home. Joy did not meet her: perhaps her children were pursuing their education out of doors, or maybe they were with her visiting some place of interest. The authority suggested that Mrs. Davies visit her again, by invitation, to assess the education Joy's children were receiving. They wanted the arrangement to be made within 14 days.

Joy replied in terms which had become her stock-in-trade:

> *"I am in receipt of your letter of February 24th. You state that your assistant, Mrs. Davies, called on me at Haddenham; but if this is the case, she did not see me and I was not aware that she had called.*

> "The education of my children is my own affair, and not that of the State. I was always given to understand that it was to avoid State interference with the liberties of individuals that we fought the last war; it does not appear to have achieved that result.
>
> "I am fully aware of my duty and responsibility as a parent and I am fulfilling these completely and in the best interests of the children. It appears to me that the well-being of the children is of infinitely more importance than any requirement of State officials. I dispute the right of any such official to interfere - and if some newspaper reports are correct, I am more than horrified at the results of their methods.
>
> "If my statement that the children are being properly educated is not sufficient to satisfy you, I would be glad if you would explain why not. Is it now a ruling in this country that the word of an individual must necessarily be treated as worthless unless investigated by an official?
>
> "I have nothing further to add to my letter of February 20th."

Clearly, Joy's position and the authorities' response lay at opposite ends of a track which was very long and full of potholes! She believed implicitly that her word had more natural weight than the authorities were prepared to give to it: they, in their turn, based their actions on an inherited suspicion of ordinary people which made them deaf and blind to any protestations of innocence and good intent. Only the unmediated observation of Joy's children by a 'professional' would suffice to convince them that she was doing all the right things - and the chances of that 'professional' agreeing with her and leaving the children entirely in her hands were, it is safe to say, remote.

She heard nothing for a while, and then two representatives of the authority came to visit her. As it happens I have taken part in similar meetings myself, and I know from that experience how hard they are on the nerves and the convictions of everybody involved. No doubt the authorities' representatives, Mr. Bartlett and Mrs. Davies, came with honest intent, but they were on Joy Baker's territory, and she read their presence as that of official predators who intended to trample on the most intimate and inviolable of all human relationships, the bond between a mother and her children. She wrote of this meeting in uncompromising terms:

> *"I could not accept in the first place that any State authority had any rights whatever over my children - such a position was contrary to all my instincts and the tenets of my own upbringing; their bland assumption of the right to hurt and destroy all I cared for infuriated me; and all the time I was talking to them I was conscious of a growing certainty that I was right - and a despairing conviction that I should never be able to prove it to a Government department. By the time they left, I realised that I was now involved in a private war."*

Having met the people who intended to direct the course of her children's education she launched in their direction a statement of her own approach to meeting the youngsters' intellectual and emotional needs. I quote it at some length because it contains as clear an exposition of how an adult might respond to children for their lifelong benefit as has ever been set down.

> "... I understand that you require proof of the education which my children are receiving in the form of 'book work' which should be submitted to Mrs. Davies for her decision as to its suitability to their age, ability and aptitude. May I then enquire what qualifications Mrs. Davies possesses which fit her to decide this? I do not refer to academic qualifications - although I should be interested to know these also, but the personal qualities of insight and understanding which would enable her to judge the ability and aptitude of my children - or any children - of whom she has no knowledge whatever? Further, I would be glad if you could inform me why you are apparently unable to accept my assurance that my children are being educated, and why you cannot leave them to be educated in peace?

> "I do not agree at all with the enforcing of a rigid timetable or the commencement of proper 'book work' at the age at which the State appears to consider it necessary. A child absorbs knowledge from the moment it is born - knowledge indisputably suited to its age, ability and aptitude - and that process continues throughout its life; but I believe a

great deal of harm is done by forcing formal instruction on children too young to be able to concentrate on or absorb facts to order. I do not agree that any formal instruction should be imposed on a child until seven or eight-years-old - although, of course, the child will learn a great deal before this age - but so far as formal education is concerned I agree with an authority writing in the Daily Telegraph recently who stated that up to that age children 'are better employed playing mothers and fathers than attending school.' My two children are learning to read - from the books of A.A. Milne (I did try teaching them with books designed for the purpose, but the children pointed out so many absurdities in the text that I ceased to use them): they are also learning to write, but this I do not want to take further until they are old enough to have a better mastery of the co-ordination between hand and eye which does not develop until a later age, and is not acquired by practice when young. I believe that too early teaching of writing is very largely responsible for the frequent establishing of an illegible adult hand. Their written work up to now is therefore limited to letters written on their own initiative to members of the family, and I have not kept school books as such. They are learning to spell accurately and to do mental arithmetic.

"They all listen to the school programmes on the wireless, the elder boy attending to every subject and giving me an account of it afterwards, the younger ones attending to the to the musical and English programmes. It is my intention to give my children the *groundwork of their education during the years between eight and twelve - reading, writing, grammar and spelling, and arithmetic; and a general introduction to history, geography, botany and biology. But I believe that the comprehensive teaching of these latter subjects should be left until a much later age, when the mind is able to grasp them fully and see facts in a clear perspective. The time spent in school in imparting quite useless instruction to minds that cannot possibly really understand it, and at best can only retain a part for a limited period, appears to me an appalling waste of the most valuable period of all human life. No child's mind is trained by such a process, much less educated - it is merely battered by it, and that although it passes for such in schools, is not and can never be education. Mathematics and chemistry I would leave altogether until and unless a child shows some leanings towards them, and languages also, which if learned at all should be learned as a chosen study, not part of a general education. The boys will learn to work with their hands in garden and workshop, and the girls in the house, as a matter of course; all team games I regard as an abomination and would not have my children participate in them. These are the lines on which I am educating my children.*

"*Your Mrs Davies asked me if I had any aim or plan in the education of my children. May I quote from the chapter on education in 'Perseus in the Wind', by Freya Stark:*

"'... I would like to have learned four things when the passing bell puts an end to schooling, and of these only one can be called intellectual. I would like to command happiness; to recognise beauty, to value death; to increase, to my capacity, enjoyment. Around the cardinal points, and inevitably attained by their attainment, I should place the conquest of fear, whose elimination must be the final aim of teachers. The rest of education deals with technical means for living, and is of secondary importance, whatever economists may say. It is chiefly because they have reversed our order and made the technical intellect supreme that we are suffering in the world today.'

"My aims are on these lines also. There are elemental things which I would teach my children, not included in the teaching of your schools - cleanliness, courtesy, and kindness, consideration for others, loyalty and gentleness and the care of those weaker than themselves; strength and courage to stand up to fear and pain; a true understanding of animal life and the natural world. And I would give them, above all things, that which is implicit in the peace of wood and field, in every springing blade of grass and the petal of every flower, in every sunrise and sunset, in the song of every wild bird - that which is beauty and happiness both, and more - that which is not knowledge but understanding of the meaning of life itself.

"May I quote again - from Keats's 'What the Thrush said':

> '*O fret not after knowledge - I have none,
> And yet my song comes native with the warmth.
> O fret not after knowledge - I have none,
> And yet the evening listens...*'
>
> "*I ask you, sir, does the evening listen to you?*"

I quote Joy at length here because it reveals the true nature of the educational programme which she had put in place for her children. Her emphasis on the subtler aims of education - the conquest of fear, the opening of the learner's mind to the awesome panorama of nature and to the social skills which are so hard to cultivate in the pressured, rigid environment of a large school - challenged the unspoken but widely accepted assumption that schooling has to be demanding and at least mildly unpleasant so that the children will learn to expect life to be harsh and frustrating when they grow up.

Her clear statement of her aims and philosophy of education were answered by nothing more than the service of another three attendance orders. She returned them to their sender, as before, in small pieces.

By this time she had moved again to Norfolk, and was staying with her parents at Brundall. The local constable delivered summonses, alleging that she had failed to send her children to the nominated schools in Buckinghamshire. Later the summonses were withdrawn and she was told that she would not have to attend court. At this point she moved yet again, in July 1954, to Yaxham, which became her permanent home.

Chapter four

A Mad World, My Masters

What happened next could only be described as horrific. We are used, in the early years of the twenty-first century, to the oppression and even the murder of children, but we comfort ourselves with the knowledge that these things happen in third-world countries, where cruelty is endemic and apparently beyond all curing. We also assume that since the nameless crimes which were uncovered in the concentration camps and punished at Nuremburg, we Europeans have turned our back for ever on the organised wrenching of children away from their parents without the very best of humane reasons.

In Yaxham, Joy received a visit from the school attendance officer. She told him that she did not intend to send her children to his schools until the autumn term. She had been thinking about whether the game was worth the candle, and she had, very tentatively, decided to explore the possibility of sending her children to a school in the next village, whose reputation was somewhat less negative than the one in Yaxham. She could not convince herself that she was wrong about school education, but the constant clashes with the law, which her middle-class instincts were certainly prompting her to uphold, were draining her nervous energy.

She put her reservations and doubts to the attendance officer, hoping they might arrive at some mutually acceptable compromise. From her point of view she was only continuing to exercise an option which had been available to her parents before the second world war. To him, she was wilfully and irrationally rejecting a provision which the state had made for her children with all the expertise that organised government assumed it alone was able to muster. The negotiation continued in a desultory way, with the attendance officer, Mr F.J.Earl, insisting that because *he* had enjoyed his time at school, and his children were, he reported, also content with their experience there, Joy ought to have no objection to sending her children through the same system. Joy took the view that just as his children were, arguably, a reflection of his approach to life and education, so hers were growing up in the mould created by her ideas and attitudes.

More attendance orders came, and were ignored. Then the local authority showed its hand in a way which ought to have been recognised as profoundly corrosive and harmful, but which expressed the anger and frustration which authority feels when someone who is supposed to uphold the rules challenges them with reason and logic, revealing the truth hidden behind all lawmaking, that even if the choices made by legislators are flawed, they cannot be criticised or opposed.

Joy had gone to Aylesbury to sort out some legal business which required her personal attendance. She could not return the same day, so she left her children in the care of a woman who occasionally did domestic work in the house.

She returned the next day, to meet the domestic help who called out, distraught, *"Don't let the car go!"*

Joy asked the driver to wait, and went into the house. She discovered that her children had been taken away the previous night by the authorities. A policewoman, several policemen, a female magistrate, and an inspector from the N.S.P.C.C. had come to the house, gained entry through a window, and woken the sleeping children. They had dressed them and, despite the protestations of the domestic helper who was looking after them, had carried them to the police car outside. They had told the domestic helper that they would leave the children at their home if, and only if, she agreed to send them to school the next day.

Clearly, she was in no position to do this, and the officials carried the Baker children off to somewhere alien, and inevitably terrifying to children who had never been separated from their mother before. They also tried to persuade the children's temporary guardian not to wait at the house for Joy's return. Fortunately, she ignored this instruction, and gave Joy all the details she could of the 'raiding party' which had abducted her children.

Joy went to the local policeman's house, but he refused to tell her where the children were. He suggested that she go to the Dereham Police Station. She did, and from there she went with a policeman to Dereham Children's Home, where she was confronted by a matron who refused to let her see David, Robin, Felicity and Wendy. Joy cried, and called out their names, whereupon the matron, and a man who was in authority, took her and threw her out, barring the door behind her.

This happened in our country, less than a generation after a war during which millions of people, of all ages, and innocent of any crime, had been seized from their homes and dragged away to exile and death by people who represented authority and claimed to be acting out of high and respectable motives. Superficially, of course, there was an infinity of difference between what happened to Joy's children, and the great deportations which tore Europe apart. The authorities in Dereham were doing what their ingrained instincts told them was the best way to achieve their goal of securing a 'proper' education for the Baker children, and we can surmise that they saw what they did as a last resort, a sort of 'nuclear option', which, though painful in the short term, would produce what they saw as the best result for the children. Yet what they did showed very clearly that they had no insight into the minds of the children.

Imbued with the widespread western European conviction that children, because they are small, are also unimportant, insignificant and trivial, the authorities saw nothing even remotely inhumane about hauling them off to what must have seemed to them like a prison. They assumed that the fear and bewilderment which the Baker children experienced would soon be forgotten, and when they got used to going to school they would come to accept the rightness of the 'short, sharp shock' administered to their mother.

Dr. Alice Miller, in her many books about childhood, insists that adults routinely forget the indignation and even sheer terror which they felt when they were children, because there is nothing else which they can safely do with their boiling emotions. They cannot hit back at their parents, for their parents outgun them many times over, so they drive their emotions out of their conscious mind, into a secret place where they fester and transform themselves into anger and violence in later life. People whose childhood did not totally distort their emotional life may still find that the hidden travails of their early experience come out as an attachment to supposedly benevolent authority, a love of intervening in the lives of young children 'for their own good'.

These interventions may induce in children a deep, bewildering anxiety, which the adults who administer them may interpret as a valuable lesson in the harshness of 'real life', as opposed to the gentleness which children are accustomed to meeting in their ordinary life as children. Adults often affect to see childhood as a golden land where everything happens for the best on a kind of sunlit upland of benevolence and calm. Since their own experience of adulthood was often fraught with anxiety and shot through with emotional crises, it is easy for them to slip into the entirely false but seductive illusion that children 'need' to be made to share some of that emotional pain as a kind of introduction to what may befall them later in life.

Whether that feeling had anything much to do with the reasons why the authorities rounded up Joy's children cannot be known with any certainty, but we must assume that, at the very least, the people who took part in the raid recognised that what they were doing would hurt the youngsters, and could traumatise them. We may presume that, like most adults, they did not recognise that their cavalier treatment of these vulnerable children would have been regarded as mere abuse if it had been carried out by anyone who was not armed with official status and some sort of professional immunity. They probably thought that they were doing something which was regrettable but necessary in order to achieve the prime purpose of the education authorities - getting children into school.

Joy refused to leave the door of the children's home where her children had been taken. She knew that if she did what her instincts were urgently telling her to do - break into the home or lash out at a representative of the authority - she would be arrested. So, realising that no-one could legally prevent her, she lay down on the front doorstep, and made ready to stay there until they let her take her children home.

Midnight came, and a little later a police officer, Inspector Barnard, arrived. As it happened, he knew Joy's father, and showed her the first kindness she had received that evening. He assured her that if she went home the children would be returned to her the next day. With great reluctance she agreed, and he took her back to her now empty home in his car.

The next day a police car collected her and took her to Dereham police station. She was confronted with a statement drawn up by the N.S.P.C.C., which she refused to sign. She wrote her own statement and signed that, She was taken back to the children's home, and reunited with her children.

She had never seen any children in such a pathetic state. Their faces were

> "stiff with terror, the pupils of their eyes fixed and contracted, and the younger ones cried hysterically long after I got them home. It was obvious that everything they had been through was branded on their minds: after being comfortably bathed and put to bed, the horror of being awakened by policemen, made to dress, and taken by force from their home; the humiliation of being stripped of all their clothes in a strange house, and being bathed and having their hair washed with carbolic soap. Felicity was even told that they next day they would cut off her beautiful long golden hair. They said they had heard me calling them in the night, but then they were picked up and carried into a room on the other side of the house, and given 'some sort of sweets', and after that they didn't remember anything more. Had this not, of course, been impossible in the Council's care, I would have assumed that that they had been drugged."

Throughout the next day the children went from hysteria to extreme exhaustion and back several times. Their reaction may have been heightened by the contrast between their experience of life until then and the horror which had been visited on them so suddenly. It took them several days to return to more or less normal. The authorities, however, did not seem to understand how deeply they had driven a wedge between themselves and their aim of getting the youngsters into school. Their system ground out yet another attendance notice. It directed Joy to send her children to Yaxham Voluntary Aided Primary School because it was 'considered suitable' for them.

Joy's problem with this authority, as with all the previous ones, revolved around the fact that civil servants generally think in broad, generalised categories, whereas she focused upon the individual needs of her children. To her, 'suitable' meant something very different from what it meant to the authorities. They assumed that 'suitable' education was the traditional daily round of the Three R's, odd periods of physical activity and occasional sessions of art and craft. Since this could be done anywhere, and with a little prudent inspection could be kept up to a modest standard of performance, the only issue between them and Joy was which school was closest to her home.

For Joy, 'suitable' had an almost infinitely more rigorous and subtle meaning. A suitable school, as far as she was concerned, would be one which respected and responded to the individual structure of her children's minds, which recognised when they were in difficulties and helped them, which gave them a voice in the running of their lives, and above all, which understood that education is for life, and that what happens to small children stays in their minds until their dying day.

Joy replied as we might expect her to:

> "Reference your letter of November 11th, I shall not be sending my children to the Yaxham Primary School as having made enquiries regarding this school I do not consider it suitable for my children. I would be glad if you would inform me how, having no knowledge whatever of the children concerned, you reach your conclusion that this school would be suitable? It was until recently my intention to send the three elder children to Mattishall School at the beginning of next term - the younger child I do not intend in any case to send to school for another year. Following, however, the events of two weeks ago, when my children suffered extreme shock and terror at the hands of local police and authorities, I am necessarily giving fresh consideration to the position. I would draw your attention to the fact that the children were told that the police took them out of their beds in the middle of the night because they had not been attending school and the woman who was in charge of them was informed that the children would be left in the home unmolested if she gave an undertaking that they would be sent to school the next day. You will doubtless appreciate that this outrage has had a serious effect on the minds of the children, and they are still suffering from its effects. I am, of course, taking up the matter in other quarters, but so far as the children's education is concerned, I can only inform you at present that they will not be attending any

school for the remainder of this term; and that next term I shall either be sending them to Mattishall School or arranging for them to receive suitable education at home."

Her relationship with the authorities was based on a dialogue of the deaf. One wonders whether either side realised that the other could not reply coherently to its case. Joy was defending her children with every particle of strength she possessed against what she saw as a a serious threat to their mental and emotional well being. The authorities had been charged with applying a law which had been constructed by the most powerful men in the land to benefit a whole class of people.

Since the authorities could not answer Joy's questions about their choice of a school for her children in a way which would have procured her co-operation, probably for no better reason than that they could not understand them, or viewed them as absurd, they continued with the procedure which had so far failed so dismally.

Almost immediately Joy received the next set of letters from the authority. It gave no evidence that anyone involved in the matter had read most of what she had written. Nothing was said about the kidnapping of her children. The only thing which mattered was that she had mentioned, very tentatively, the possibility of sending her children to Mattishall Primary School. This was ruled out by the fact that the school was two and a half miles from Joy's home, and it seemed likely that the authority would have to provide some means of transport to take the children to and from school. That would have been unthinkable, of course.

The whole question was put before the Minister of Education, no less, and Joy was given an opportunity to make representations to him about her case. She replied, in her usual trenchant terms, that although she had been contemplating sending her children to Mattishall, since the authorities had raided her home in her absence and dragged them off to a children's home she would be keeping the youngsters' with her and educating them herself. She added:,

> "I may say that I regard it as my duty to consider, above any other consideration, the health, happiness and well-being of my children, irrespective of the impositions of any State-created 'authority' (which in any case I do not acknowledge), and I shall bring up and educate my children in accordance with my own ideas and beliefs as my parents did, and their parents and their parents before them. I do not regard the education provided by the State as fit for any child who is to grow up an intelligent, sound and individual adult, particularly when it comes to the children being forcibly removed from their home, at night, by the police, in an attempt to enforce their attendance at a State School. I shall be obliged if you will so inform the Minister."

As we have seen, Joy had some very specific ideas about schools and what they did to children. We might reasonably ask why the authority did not spend at least a little time addressing itself to her arguments and questions. Perhaps the simplest explanation is that education authorities tend to consist largely of people who have been teachers, and as such aspire to being members of a profession. In order to be a 'professional' one has to possess knowledge which cannot be obtained by outsiders, without a long period of training and assessment. Teachers have to have a body of knowledge to teach to their pupils, but once they have mastered that there is very little they have to know which could not be imparted to any person of ordinary intelligence in a few weeks, maybe even less.

The techniques of teaching are more about securing the attention of large groups of children, disabling their individual learning techniques, and making them concentrate on a single area of interest, decided for them by their teacher. It is not difficult to imagine the effect produced in the minds of senior education officials by the suggestion that an untrained, albeit suitably middle-class. woman could provide the education for her children which they, and only they, were supposed to know how to give them.

I do not intend to suggest - for I have no way of knowing - that they believed she was totally incompetent. She was certainly articulate and from the general class of people who became schoolmistresses. Perhaps they even thought that it really might be just a question of her allowing someone from the Education Office to come to her house, sniff about for a little while and then report back that she was doing more or less what their teachers were doing, albeit in a more unstructured and discursive way. Yet she could not allow that to happen because if she did, her whole philosophy of education would have been under threat as soon as the authority's representative began to make 'helpful' suggestions, which he or she would undoubtedly have expected Joy to incorporate into her practice. Authority representatives had no other model of education other than school on which to base their 'advice', and Joy knew that she was working in a way which had no element of enforced didacticism in it, no 'training', no mass, indiscriminate socialisation.

She had a canny realisation that there was little room in the minds of officialdom for free children doing what pleased them and getting the knowledge they wanted to have. Certainly, try as she might, she had not succeeded in persuading the authority to reveal the body of knowledge and the framework of ideas by which they assumed children should be educated.

She tried again. In answer to another request that she allow inspectors into her home she wrote:

"With reference to your letter of March 26th, I am prepared to agree to your Inspector calling to examine my children provided that you give me satisfactory replies to the following questions: on what grounds have the Education Committee decided that Yaxham School is suitable for the four children in question, none of whom they have ever seen; and what qualifications will the Inspector possess that will enable him or her to assess the ability, aptitude and educational needs of these children in a brief visit, more beneficially

than can the parent who has studied the children throughout their lives; and provided that I may be permitted to visit Yaxham School which the Committee consider suitable for my children (without prior notice having been given to those in charge) and inspect the children at work, the preparation of meals, and the lavatories.

"I await your reply with interest."

The authority replied with yet another threat of court proceedings. Joy was clearly not going to be allowed to inspect Yaxham School. The Clerk of the Dereham Magistrates' Court telephoned her father, pleading with him to use his influence towards persuading Joy to send her children to school. If she did not, he insisted, they would be taken away from her.

This flagrant piece of premature adjudication may well have been designed to force Joy's hand, but it seemed to stem from a deep sense of bewilderment about the relationship between ordinary householders and authority. Children had always gone to school: parents had always sent them there, and in the tiny minority of cases where feckless, usually dirty and ill-favoured families had not made their children go to school, there was a recognised, well-understood procedure in which the adults appeared in court, were named in the local press and fined, and sent to prison if they did not pay.

The children would either be taken to school by the Wag Man, later to be known as the Attendance Officer or, even later, the Educational

Welfare Officer, or sent to a children's home, and that would be the end of that. But none of this was supposed to happen to articulate, cultivated parents like Joy. They were thought to be ambitious for their children, and recognise the value of knowledge, industry and 'discipline', which usually implied doing things one would rather not do in order to learn that life in the adult world was certain to be hard and unrelenting. It was assumed that they would agree with the whole package of experiences which made up the school experience, and would have more pressing things to to do with their time than trying to recreate them at home.

Joy spoke to her parents about the Magistrates' Clerk's telephone call. It turned out that her father had said that he could not influence her decision in any way.

The very next day four summonses arrived, one per child. Joy took them to her solicitor, Mr. James Hipwell. At first he tried to persuade her not to contest the case. He expressed the opinion that she would only be knocking her head against a brick wall. Her reply was typical of the campaigner she had become:

"Well, I might dislodge a few bricks."

Mr. Hipwell, finding his initial advice spurned, did what he could to ease Joy's passage through the Courts. He asked for an adjournment to allow for the preparation of the case. He also persuaded the Authorities to allow Joy to inspect the local schools, in exchange for which she would be prepared to allow the Inspectors to visit her children.

Chapter five

Quis Custodiet?
(Who Will Guard the Guards?)

The inspectors arrived. The senior inspector, Mr. Greenwood, and his junior colleague, Mr. Thompson, insisted on seeing the children alone. Mr. Thompson took the girls into the nursery and Mr. Greenwood closeted himself with the boys in the dining room.

Mr. Thompson was a Scotsman, and the girls found it very difficult to understand what he was saying to them. They were used to the broad, flat vowels of Norfolk, and their ears strained to make sense of the Celtic sounds with which his speech was peppered. He made some effort to be friendly, but the poor communication between him and the girls hampered his attempts to discover what they had learned.

Mr. Greenwood had 'a grin like a crocodile' and halfway through his examination of the boys, David came out of the dining room very white, and went into the lavatory. Nervous tension always produced physical sickness and diarrhoea in him, Joy recorded. When he returned the inspector told him that the time he was allotted for the task he had been given, writing a letter, was up. He was not allowed to finish it. Meanwhile Robin was too terrified even to begin to do what Mr. Greenwood wanted him to do, and was sent from the room in tears. The visit showed clearly how easy it is to manipulate meetings with children so that they show whatever the adult wishes them to.

A different approach, based on asking the children respectfully to show what they had learned to do would have had a far more positive result. But inspectors do not liberate children, they test them. Their function is to find out how closely performance matches up with expectation, and that requires them to have the narrowest possible view of the world. Its limits must be the curriculum, and the assumption that nothing outside it can be of any real value.

The next day Joy did what she had wanted to do for a very long time. She went to inspect the two local schools, Yaxham and Mattishall. She was taken into an infants' class where she found what later generations of school critics have come to expect:

> "a handful of tinies, some of whom were under five, sitting in rows at little tables, staring at large A.B.C.s with lack-lustre eyes. They had very much the look of small captive animals, their initial fear dulled by repetition, all animation and feeling wiped from their faces - yet I am sure they were not like that at home."

Joy asked to see the lavatories. The teacher who was showing her the school was not sure that this was a good idea *"But they're outside, you know - and it's raining - you'll get so wet..."* Joy asked something which seemed to her blindingly obvious, but which had clearly occurred to nobody else involved with setting up and running the school: *"But these little children have to use them in all weathers?"*

"Well, yes..." replied the teacher. Joy went across the playground and saw the lavatories. She was not impressed.

After that she was taken into the main class, where all the other children in the school had their lessons. Her reaction to this is worth recording in detail because it shows very clearly the difference between what might be called the ordinary expectations which parents have of teachers, and the ideas which an individual who has thought carefully about education might decide upon if she had been brought up to respect the children and not the adults set over them:

"I was shown the books the children were reading - the type of boys' and girls' adventure stories my brother and I had read at home occasionally, but not what I would have chosen as examples of good English or good literature.

"I was shown exercise books containing essays and other written work by the children - and was appalled to find actual errors of fact, apparently taught, and marked as correct, by the teacher. 'Badgers live in forests', one child wrote; but they don't necessarily, they live in woods, fields, even in large gardens - I have met one crossing a country road, many miles from a forest of any kind. Country children should learn nature study from personal experience and observation, and books by field naturalists, not by copying out meaningless

sentences in class. 'Mobile' means 'easily moved', another child had written. All right so far as it goes perhaps, but it does not go far enough; and what is that child going to make of hearing that someone has a 'mobile face'?

"It is obvious that insufficient importance is placed in schools today on the proper and effective use of words; and from the start I wanted my children to learn and understand all their different shades of meaning, and use them with force and expression. Children normally do this naturally, until school teaching imposes rigid rules. It would not have passed in a school essay, but we all knew exactly what David meant when - not having met the word 'fusty' - he exclaimed at teatime, 'This butter tastes like old sheds!'

"I was also struck by the extreme uniformity of the children's handwriting. Without looking at the names on the covers it was impossible to tell that the exercise books belonged to different children; and all were written in what in my childhood was known as 'an uneducated hand' - examples of which can be seen on the walls of almost every public building in the country."

She was then shown the kitchen, though it was not one where fresh food was prepared. The authority was one of those which supplied its schools with food cooked in a central kitchen, stowed in vacuum containers and distributed in such a way as to arrive in time for the children's midday meal.

As one who has eaten such food I can testify that it was unpalatable because it was never, ever hot enough, and much of it tasted, in David Baker's vivid phrase, 'like old sheds'. It was probably the best which could be made of a bad job, in view of the financial constraints of the period, but Joy was clear in her own mind that *"... children should have freshly cooked, attractively served meals, not warmed-up food carried round in a van."*

She left Yaxham School deeply unimpressed, and went on to Mattishall, a larger school with larger classes. The teacher who showed Joy round seemed proud of the fact that some of her five-year-olds were reading newspapers. Joy was not impressed. In her opinion newspapers were not suitable reading for five-year-olds. One might wonder just how a teacher would set about getting a child in the first year of school to read the *Times*, or even the *Daily Mirror*. I enjoyed the latter at an age not much greater than those children. However, I did not spend much time on the articles. I preferred the cartoons - *Pip, Squeak and Wilfred* and *Chad*, the lugubrious watcher over the wall with his endless 'Wot no ...!' slogans.

Children can certainly get pleasure from sharing some aspects of adult life, like the newspapers, but I should be suspicious of a school which used them as a teaching aid with infant-age pupils. They are, after all, written specifically for adults, and often fairly sophisticated adults at that. Perhaps the teacher was one of those who saw education purely in terms of 'performance', the ability of pupils to do exceptional things.

A pupil was asked to read to Joy:

"The book on the desk in front of him was one containing stories alternated with pages of exercises and lists of words. Three times he started reading on the wrong page. At last the teacher showed him the start of the story they had been reading, and he read it perfectly - also mechanically and without expression. It was obvious that he understood neither the layout of the book nor the meaning of the story he read."

Joy then noticed that one of the children who was laying the tables for dinner - these were the same tables as they had used for their lessons - was carrying some spoons by their bowls. *"Perhaps you could teach them to hold spoons and forks by the handles",* she suggested. The lavatories, at the far end of the playground, and viewed from a decent distance, completed her tour.

The next day she appeared in Dereham Magistrates' Court. The bench consisted of six people, five men and one woman. I am in no position to comment on the efficacy of justice dispensed by lay people, but the fact that the chairman, Major Wormald, was also the chairman of the Governors of a Girls' High School, a governor of Dereham Secondary Modern School, and a manager of two other schools might have cast doubt on his impartiality. Perhaps the simple truth is that only Joy saw the conflict between herself and the school system as a question of education. For the authorities she was simply another criminal parent to be processed and forced to comply.

The course of events was rehearsed by Mr. Brighton, the Norfolk County Council's assistant solicitor and Mr. Earl, the Senior Welfare Officer of the Norfolk Education Committee. They laid before the magistrates the attempts which they had made to get Joy to send her children to a school. They described the children, - David, aged nine, Robin, aged eight, Felicity, aged seven and Wendy aged six. - as 'healthy, bright and intelligent', but in spite of their mother's closely argued and extensive account of her educational ideas, they were not prepared to say that she was giving them an adequate and appropriate education. They had made enquiries, as the law, in their estimation, required them to do, and they had not seen anything which, they felt, entitled them to accept Joy's representations.

Then Mr. Greenwood, one of the inspectors who had visited the children, was called to give evidence. It was clear that he had gone to the visit armed with a very clear idea about how much children were supposed to have learned by a given age. He was prepared to concede that the young Bakers were 'perfectly delightful', but his examination of them led him to the conclusion that they were behind where they were supposed to be, or more accurately, where they would probably have been if they had been sent to school. He had asked them to read, write and do arithmetic, and they had not been able to do even the relatively simple tasks he had given them.

Joy's own testimony set before the court the simple facts that she was a married woman living with her children at a house called the Rookery in Yaxham. She contended that she was giving them a suitable education, and in any case she did not think children should go to school, if at all, until they were at least ten-years-old.

She went on to say that her children had been removed from their home in the night by uniformed police, and this had had a serious effect on them. She pointed out that the half-hour period which Mr. Greenwood had allotted to David for him to write a letter was in fact not much more than five minutes, because he had been so nervous that he had gone to the toilet and spent most of his time there. It was small wonder, then, that he had produced very little work, since Mr. Greenwood had removed the paper from him and not allowed him to make up for lost time.

She had taught the children to speak clearly, to have good manners, to be clean, courteous, considerate and gentle, all of which she considered to be more important than the Three Rs.

Mr. Brighton cross-examined her, and she told him that she taught the children what they were ready to learn. She did not, she said, force anything on them, neither did she keep anything from them. For instance, they had been told exactly why the inspectors were coming to visit them.

The members of the bench questioned her and she told them that she wanted her children to 'develop as they are, and not as others think they should be'. She wanted them to grow up as individuals and not part of a mass.

The magistrates retired, and when they returned the chairman said that the bench was not satisfied that the children were getting sufficient education at home. They fined Joy £1 for each child.

When she rejoined her children in the anteroom where they had been waiting in case the magistrates wished to see them, she found them sitting in tense silence. It transpired that a policeman had told them that if they did not keep quiet he would 'get a gun and shoot them'.

The press besieged Joy's home, and she told them that in spite of the magistrates' decision, she would not be sending her children to school.

Such an episode would probably not happen today. As a society we have come to realise that questions of education are not as simple to answer as people thought 50 years ago. Nowadays a policeman would almost certainly think twice before threatening children with shooting to keep them quiet, and a visiting inspector would probably give more weight to the calmness and sociability of the children he was observing than Mr. Greenwood did.

The conviction still persists, however, that there are things which children of a given age must be taught or their education is a failure. No amount of experience seems to dislodge from the mind of adults the idea that schooling is sovereignly about teaching and learning, and that everything else, the social and emotional aspects of life when one is a child and the feelings which arise in the minds of pupils when they meet with pressures from the school environment which they cannot understand or endure, are either completely irrelevant or only to be considered if they can fit into the basic fabric of a traditional school. So, for example, we still have bullying, because the measures which might put an end to it are not capable of being set up in a large, hierarchical institution where adults rule and children rarely tell them the unvarnished truth.

The need for children to make decisions democratically so that they learn the arts of negotiation and debate is unimaginably dangerous to the average authoritarian teacher, so it does not figure in the planning of most schools. In short, education is still almost entirely governed by the needs, emotional and practical, of the adults who use schools as day-prisons for their children, and the other adults who make a living from herding those children from class to class and lesson to lesson.

The next stage in Joy's journey through the courts was her appeal against the magistrates' verdict. This took place at the Shirehall in Norwich.

Joy was allowed to sit at the solicitors' table, as she was conducting her own defence, but she was intimidated by being in a place where the most important aspects of her life, and the lives of her children, were to be decided by professionals with their own language and ways of thinking, over which she seemed to have little or no control.

Her ordeal began when Mr. Robert Ives, the barrister engaged by the council, opened his case by saying that if the appeals were dismissed he had instructions to apply for an order that Joy's children be brought before the Juvenile Court.

It is hard for readers in the early years of the twenty-first century to absorb the enormity of that proposal. We still have Juvenile Courts, and we still bring children and young people before them, but generally only for reasons which can be identified as 'criminal'. We still regard non-attendance at school as somehow reprehensible, but we have managed to discern that when children are well-behaved, calm, gentle, and curious it makes no sense to wrench them away from their home and familiar surroundings simply in order to put them through a process which we have come to think of as 'normal'. We have learned to value children more highly than the rulers of education did in Joy's day.

The process of admitting children into the full enjoyment of human rights is not yet completed. We still find, for example, that the majority of British parents want the right to hit their children by way of punishment. But we have, at least, abandoned the generalised contempt for children which enabled earlier generations to do more or less anything to them, from physical and sexual abuse to commercial exploitation and organised ill-treatment masquerading as 'care'. Joy's uncompromising commitment to her children, and her challenge to an establishment which saw no reason to consider any system of thought other than its own laid the groundwork for reforms which are beginning to be seen positively, even though political concerns seems to stand in the way of their realisation.

Mr. Ives went over what had been said and done up to the time of the appeal, and then called Mr. Earl, who gave the same general line of testimony as he had at the magistrates' court. Joy rose to cross-examine him. She began with the question which she had already asked a dozen times: in view of the fact that the committee had never seen her children, how could they determine that Yaxham School was suitable for them?

His reply was the only one he could have given, under the circumstances: Yaxham School was the one which children living in that area were expected to attend. Joy pursued the matter:

> *"It is not then really a decision that this school is the most suitable, but that it is the nearest school?"*

Mr. Earl, for whom a limited measure of sympathy is perhaps appropriate, could not undermine the system he served by agreeing with her. He merely repeated his former answer: *"It is the school considered most suitable."*

Joy pressed on:

> *"The question of considering 'age, ability and aptitude' is therefore pure nonsense? In fact, all the authority care about is not that the*

children should receive suitable education, but that they should attend the nearest school?"

Mr. Earl replied, as he had to:

"Yaxham School is regarded by the authority as the proper school for children up to the age of 11 in that area. It is considered suitable for the ability and aptitude of these children."

Joy asked: *"Although their actual individual ability and aptitude are not known to the authority?"* and received the inevitable, weary answer: *"It is considered suitable."*

The reader should, perhaps, find this exchange disturbing. Education was, and still is, supposed to be a subtle and humane profession, requiring much training and insight into the minds of children. In its organised form it took, in my day, three years to train for, and it has since become the basis of a full-blown degree course. Yet Joy revealed, through her questioning, that far from incorporating a careful diagnosis of each pupil's needs and susceptibilities, even the most modern kind of education was no more than a process by which a stream of conventional knowledge was played over each generation of the nation's children in the hope that some of it, at least, would stick.

No attention had been paid to how individual pupils reacted to this process, and nothing could be done within its compass which was even remotely responsive to the unique world-vision of each child, unless it could be conveniently organised around the 'delivery' of the common curriculum.

Joy's next question concerned her own status as an educator:

> "In the magistrates' court my solicitor put it to you that I was an educated woman. You did not agree, but said that I was an intelligent person."

Mr Earl agreed.

> "I attended school for eight years. Are you saying that an intelligent person who has attended school for eight years may still not be educated?"

Mr. Earl declined to comment.

Joy continued with what ought to have been, but was not recognised as, the destruction of Mr. Earl's case:

> "You say you do not think a child can be educated in isolation. What do you call isolation?"
>
> "To be properly educated a child needs to be with other children."
>
> "Do you honestly consider that a child can be taught properly - let alone educated, which is a different thing altogether - in a large class?"

Mr. Earl was never at a loss for a well-tried and entirely thought free answer: *"I think a great part of education for a child consists of it being in a class."*

The headmistress of Yaxham School was brought in to confirm that Joy had not sent her children there. Asked whether she wanted her to remain Joy said she did not have anything to say to her, and the headmistress returned to her school.

Then it was the turn of Mr. Greenwood, the senior inspector. He gave very similar evidence to that which he had given in the magistrates' court. He made one point which drew a surprised rejoinder from Joy. He said that the children had been nervous during his visit 'because Joy had told them the reason for the inspectors' visit.' She asked him whether he agreed with her doing this, and he replied that 'it was not necessary'.

She hit back hard:

"Then you are telling the court, on oath, Mr. Greenwood, that on some occasions you think it is better not to tell the truth?"

Clearly unable to pick his way through a moral argument with which he had never been faced before, Mr. Greenwood spluttered and grimaced before muttering something about how this situation was different. He did not explain how.

Joy pulled to pieces his conduct of the visit, He had said that it was 'quite delightful', but he acknowledged that the children had been 'shy'. Joy challenged him to accept that they had, in fact, been frightened witless. He denied this, and saw no reason to attribute David's long visit to the lavatory to diarrhoea brought on by sheer nervousness. He did not think that the boys' uncertainty had anything to do with the fact that he had asked them to write about 'anything', instead of giving them a choice of subjects. He had clearly forgotten what it was like to be a small child (I vividly remember the bewilderment I felt when asked, at the age of seven or eight, to 'write a story'. I suspect he would have felt the same at that age).

Joy asked Mr. Greenwood about the strange conclusion he had come to about Felicity's reading. She had not followed the words she had been reading with her finger, but for some reason had pointed to other words as she read. He had concluded that she was not actually reading. What else she might have been doing, since she was speaking the words printed on the page, he did not say, but he was sure that she was not reading.

Did he realise, Joy asked, that his assistant, who had examined the girls, had a strong Scots accent, which made his words difficult to understand? Mr. Greenwood thought not. It was becoming clear that what he expected from children was nothing remotely like what Joy was labouring to get from hers. He could only reiterate that they had not reached 'the standard'.

He could see nothing else in them, no kindness or gentleness, no refinement of manners or speech, no outgoing attitude or enthusiasm for life which could be weighed in the balance against the fact that they could not do certain things which their schooled contemporaries seemed to be able to do. He could not fathom Joy's argument that children would learn things more surely if they were allowed to learn them as and when they saw the need, instead of when those things happened to appear in the school curriculum.

After Mr. Greenwood came Mr. Thompson, who described himself as an 'educational psychologist.' He had also been present at the visit to Joy's home, and it had been his broad Scots accent which the girls had found so difficult to understand. The same accent produced a ripple of laughter in the courtroom when he asserted that his degree had been conferred by 'Edinburr-rrgh Univairr-sity', but Joy found his testimony broadly fair, and did not question him further.

It was now Joy's turn to put her case. It is worth quoting at length because it is as clear and winning a statement of the aims of learner-managed education as one might wish to hear, and evidence, if any more were needed, that education authorities are pursuing radically different aims in the conduct of their schools from those which a humane parent, who had thought hard about what her children needed, would set out to attain. She said:

"I am not sending my children to school because I am educating them at home. I have my own views on education, and I believe schools do a great deal of harm. I maintain that it is wrong to separate upbringing and scholastic instruction, and that education should be the combining of both in the secure surrounding of the child's home. I regard education as a preparation for life rather than sessions of formal instruction, which are often incomprehensible to the minds of children and

given in surroundings inevitably uncongenial and frequently repellent to the sensitive child.

"No two of my four children are alike, and each requires and receives an individual approach which would be impossible in any school, where the tendency is to stamp out individuality.

"I do not agree that formal instruction should start at five unless the mind of the child is obviously ready for it. I maintain that seven is the earliest age that any normal child should be required to start taking lessons as such, and I understand that this view is supported by experts. I believe it is correct that our present Queen started lessons at that age. I would be interested to know whether the Education Authorities regard her as having been inadequately educated.

"At seven I have started teaching my children reading, writing and elementary arithmetic, and awakening an interest in drawing, nature study and music, as and when they showed an interest in these things. Also as part of their education they have from an early age been taught and encouraged to carry out various aspects of housework and other domestic duties.

"The elder boy listens to all the instructional programmes on the wireless and is in this way receiving tuition in history, geography, natural history and, at his own wish, other more advanced subjects. I have intentionally withheld any more extensive instruction in

history, and, to a certain extent, in geography, because I believe these to be subjects which if they are to be properly understood and seen in true perspective, rather than as a series of disconnected episodes and facts, can only be absorbed by a more mature mind. It is my intention, therefore, that the children's study of geography should be intensified between the ages of ten and fifteen, and that they should read history as a whole when they are capable of understanding it between the ages of fifteen and twenty. In my experience the mind of a child finds it easier to comprehend the functions of the natural world and the nature of the Universe than the complicated political events which constitute a great deal of history."

It must have been strange and indeed a little unnerving to hear such radical theorising about education from a quietly spoken, plainly middle-class mother. Her decision to delay the beginning of formal instruction was probably born of intuition rather than any great amount of research, but it validly challenged the prevailing wisdom that schooling should start at five.

I do not know for certain why this early age was chosen, but my suspicion is that it was a utilitarian decision based on the realisation that nineteenth century childhood, among the majority of families at least, came to an end as soon as the child could do a day's work and contribute to the family's income. If the government intended to administer anything like an extended education to the rising generation of young Britons it would have to start young, and cram the whole programme into about five or six years, before the pressure of economic reality forced them to let the children go into the factories and workshops.

It is desperately sad that no-one has had the wit to reconsider the beginning of education as conditions changed, and it became possible to postpone the end of it until the child had reached an ever greater age. Thus the idea came into being and flourished, that education through schooling is a great social benefit, and the more of it we can put our children through the better all our lives will be, and it matters not whether the youngster reacts to it with enthusiasm or sullen resistance.

Joy continued:

"The children have not been required to practise handwriting to any great extent, as I believe it is only in the later years, between ten and fifteen, that a child acquires fully the necessary co-ordination between hand and eye required to write well; I am anxious that my children should acquire a good individual hand, and not learn at an early age the uniform 'uneducated' hand common to the majority of their contemporaries attending the State schools. In view of this the greater part of the children's instruction and work has been oral."

She offered for the attention of the Appeals Committee examples of each child's handwriting. She had given them a poem, 'The Wild Flower's Prayer', to copy out:

'Keep us from the careless boots
Trampling on our tender shoots,

> And from those who take for granted
> That every flower can be transplanted...'

She continued:

> *"The children are taught to speak properly; proper table manners; personal cleanliness; and the qualities of courtesy, gentleness and consideration for others, which I regard as more important than routine school subjects."*

She went on to tell of the gardening, nature study and farm work which the children did, and the visits they made to art galleries, museums, films of educational interest and orchestral concerts which they had visited. They had also learned elementary first aid. and often took part in discussions about the things they had learned when they felt they needed to raise questions:

> *"The primary purpose of education during the early years - when a child is not capable of absorbing any quantity of dry facts - is to awaken and interest the mind, so that it is readily receptive of the facts that it can and will absorb without any difficulty in later years. All the education given to a child up to the age of seven or eight in school could be assimilated by any intelligent adult in a matter of a few weeks."*

I suspect that her estimates of what could be learned by an intelligent adult were conservative: personally I incline to the belief that the entire curriculum of the primary school could be imparted to an average 13-year-old in a month if he or she were disposed to learn it.

Joy pressed on with her entirely reasonable defence of her scheme of education:

> "No-one is expected or advised by health experts to force food down a child's throat because it has reached an age when a text book says it should have that type or quantity of food. In feeding a child you judge what is required by its consumption of what it is given and its apparent need for more. Why then should the mind be forcibly fed? A child's mind and body grow and develop without referring to textbooks - or consulting education authorities. It is as senseless to put a child day after day in a classroom and give it instruction, nine-tenths of which its mind is not ready to receive, and call the result education, as it would be to seat a child at table and surround it with plates of food which it could not digest, and maintain it was properly fed."

Her next contention, that children to not show any real interest in what they are taught, and retain little or none of it, might strike the average reader as overstated. We are certainly used to seeing young children apparently learning and showing evidence of having stowed what they have been taught away in their minds until at least the end-of-year exams, but it is worth asking the question: is this evidence of real learning? As a French language teacher I have often met with children who knew by heart any number of verb-paradigms, of the pattern 'Je suis = I am / tu es = you (singular, familiar) are/ il est = he or it is/ elle est = she or it (feminine) is', and so forth, but who could no more construct for themselves a simple sentence using the correct part of the conjugation than fly in the air. They knew discrete parts of the language, having been given them to memorise for a test, but they could not put them to any useful purpose.

This is notoriously true of language-teaching and learning, because those involved know that the learners and the teacher already have a perfectly serviceable language with which to exchange thoughts, and so the pupils frequently see no pressing reason to say things in any other language, but I should not be surprised if teachers of most other subjects could find analogous examples in their own fields of pupils learning things to get high marks in exams but never using them for anything else. Joy's critique of education may be disturbing, but it is at least defensible.

Joy went on to challenge the whole concept of 'standards' - pieces of learning or manifestations of maturity which children are expected to have mastered by a given stage in their development. We are, perhaps, all familiar with the way in which the mothers of young children vie with each other in telling of their children's usually precocious mastery of walking, talking, tying shoelaces and the like. They seem to enjoy having a child who does something before all the other children. Yet anyone who thinks about this harmless but pointless activity will quickly realise that within a very short space of time the differences between their children will have largely disappeared, or rather transformed themselves into the individual traits which compose their unique personality. Worrying about what children do when they are 5, 6 and

7, has little or no effect on what they do when they are 18, 19 or 20.

Joy had also noticed that even when her children seemed to be 'behind' their peers who went to school, when they finally mastered a given area of knowledge they were much more capable of using it than most schoolchildren. She said:

> "... David and Robin did not talk until they were four, but at that age they started to do so with the clarity and range of words that you would expect in a child of seven or eight.
>
> "My children have been slow to develop in almost every way, but they have developed well. They have learned gradually, but they have learned thoroughly. Everything they have been taught is alive knowledge, not dead teacher's words in their minds. They are ready and eager to go on learning, whereas too many children in school have lost interest in learning because they associate it with the dullness and boredom of school instruction, and have ceased to regard the assimilation of knowledge as a perennially exciting part of life. I maintain that for a child up to ten, an alive mind seeking and absorbing knowledge of its own free will is a far greater educational achievement than a bored mind stuffed with uninteresting facts which are never related to daily life at all."

Joy went on to elaborate this argument by referring to the different rates at which her children had learned reading and writing. The inspectors had been worried by the fact that Wendy could not write numbers. They believed

Quis custodiet? 73

that a girl who had reached her age should be able to do this. Joy knew that she would learn in her own good time, and had made no plans to teach her until she was ready. Joy's other daughter, Felicity, had made faster progress, learning the alphabet in ten minutes, not from Joy but from her older brother David.

The heart of Joy's case against the authorities was simply that she was content to let her children grow at the rate which nature had created for them, developing harmoniously as they experienced individual interaction with their surroundings, whilst they, the officials, could not free themselves from the conviction that if children do not all grow up at roughly the same speed there is something wrong either with them or with their parents - probably both - which must be remedied by clever professionals at school.

She was doing no more than echo what Edmond Holmes, the Chief Inspector of Schools who retired in 1910, wrote in his powerful critique of the school system, *What is and What Might Be,* that schoolteachers spend their time 'doing the children's development for them'. She had grasped a principle of education which had been discovered before her by A. S. Neill, who provided lessons but refused to force children to go to them. It was that every single child there has ever been has constructed his or her own mentality, using the unique blend of experiences and thought processes offered by his or her surroundings. The supposedly 'successful' ones are simply those who managed to react positively and healthily to the lessons thrust upon them by their teachers. The rest, the disaffected and apparently philistine young people who reject school and its schemes of learning are not less capable intellectually, rather they find themselves constitutionally at odds with imposed learning and cannot use it to build their mind.

History abounds with such people, and records that they had as much to do with human progress as any 'academic' person, provided only that they were able at some stage in their lives to find someone who had transmissible skills and was willing to impart them to another.

It is worth remembering that Stonehenge was built, the archaeologists tell us, by people many of whom were in their teens and early twenties - human beings had short, active lives in those days. The skill-set which enabled men to quarry stone in Wales, shape it, transport it to southern England and erect it with pinpoint accuracy at the precise place where the summer solstice was seen and celebrated was, I would contend, at least as rigorous and difficult to acquire as any modern technology, yet whole communities of young people readily adapted their lives to the need they perceived they had to build their temple. Some, no doubt, were skilled craftsmen, others more adapted to pulling and dragging, yet others gifted for planning and projecting ideas into the future. They did not, I imagine, throw tantrums or ask moodily what use the learning which they had to do might be. The need for it was self-evident. Modern schoolchildren often fail to see what use their study is supposed to be because it is detached from the immediate course of real life.

The simple truth behind all good education is that learning has to be a response to interest or felt need. Most schooling is about what interests teachers, parents and adults in general. That is why it fails so many of its young learners.

The hearing groped its way towards its end. Joy presented her arguments clearly and with a measure of articulation which would, I imagine, have induced respect in the authorities if they had been listening. She drew her submission to a close with some trenchant words:

> *"The Education Authority has stressed that these proceedings have been taken against me for the children's own welfare - but I would point out that the Education Authority can neither know nor care anything about these individual children, whereas I who am asking only to be allowed to continue to devote my life to their welfare do know and do care. Does this court maintain that the Authority's view must be right, and that of the individual must be wrong?*
>
> *"I submit that the Act allows some freedom to the individual, and that the education I am giving my children is education suitable to their age, ability, and aptitude within the meaning of the Act; and I claim the right to hold and act on my own views in the matter of the education of my children.*
>
> *"It has been established by Mr. Greenwood's own evidence that my methods have been in*

no way detrimental to my children. I submit that what the Education Authority think my methods may bring about in later life is not evidence.

"I therefore ask you to allow my appeal, and take the claws of the Education Authority out of my children, so that they may continue to live and learn in peace."

She had been on her feet for the best part of three hours, and was naturally exhausted. Her heart sank when the chairman began to speak:

"We have considered the evidence before us and we are not satisfied..."

Time stood still:

"...that the Education Committee has complied with the full requirements of the Education Act. The Committee should have made their enquiries into the education being given to these .children before the School Attendance Orders were made; but these enquiries were not made until after the making of the orders.

"Mrs. Baker has argued her case with great ability. We do not propose to express an opinion as to the education which these children are receiving. The appeals will be allowed and the Attendance Orders discharged."

The Chairman then added words which were to be significant later: *"You do appreciate, Mrs. Baker, that this is a technical point."* The attendance orders were 'discharged', whatever that may have meant to the authorities, but unlike the rule which normally governs criminal cases, that a finding of not guilty cannot be reversed or revised, this tribunal's constitution seems to have included a provision that if the accused parent managed to escape from its toils once, the authorities could have a second chance to impose their ideas of education.

Joy knew that her freedom from interference was temporary. For a short while she even contemplated looking for a school, somewhere, to which she could send her children with a good conscience. She concluded that even if such a school existed it would almost certainly have been a private school, which she could not have afforded.

She does not appear to have known about Summerhill, whose fees tend to be at the low end of the scale, but anyway, I suspect that, whilst she might have agreed with its beliefs about children and their needs, she would probably have been quietly appalled by Neill's acceptance of what he tended to think of as the 'bandit stage' of their development. He meant, of course, the years before adolescence, when children are largely ruled by their impulses, and are capable of creating great, often joyous, but also chaotic flights of fancy, which can be noisy, disturbing and productive of vast amounts of rubbish.

Chapter six

The Authorities Counterattack.

Joy's programme of learning continued without disturbance for six months. In February 1956 her third son, Hugh, was born, and in March she moved to Heath Farm House in Thuxton. In May Dr. Lincoln Ralphs, the Chief Education Officer for Norfolk, wrote to her to ask if she wanted any help with the eldest boy, David's, education. The letter was couched in civil terms and she responded, with equal civility, that she did not. Joy realised that the uneasy truce between her and the authorities was coming to an end.

In June Mr. Earl reappeared at her door, asking whether David was at school, and what plans she had for the other children's education. Clearly nothing she had said in court or to the press had made any real impression upon him. Joy told him that nothing had changed and that she would not submit to being questioned by him.

At this point the effects of illness offered the family an opportunity to show anyone with the broadness of mind to realise it that far from being sequestered from real life the Baker children had been thoroughly prepared for it by their education. David caught measles, and as soon as he was well again, the rest of the family caught it. David was just 11-years-old, but he managed to maintain the household and everyone in it with an aplomb and competence which one does not usually associate with preteen children. He called the doctor, did the shopping, cooked meals, prepared feeds for baby Hugh and brought him to his mother when he needed changing. He collected medicines from the doctor's surgery and generally saw to the family's needs, working from six in the morning until ten at night.

We expect adults to be capable of shouldering family responsibilities such as these, but I dare say that even in the early twenty-first century most people would hesitate to believe that an 11 year-old boy, even a moderately intelligent one, could run a household for a week without losing control of the situation.

We load childhood with a vast burden of negative assumptions which bear no relationship to what individual children, faced with the need to perform even difficult tasks, can do. Schools, in particular, can only continue as they are at the moment as long as their pupils are assumed to be incompetent and immature. Capable, wise children would imperil the essential balance of power in schools, because they would demand, rightly, a voice in their own affairs, and a natural authority over the process they were being put through.

Joy Baker's children were already beginning to show that, freed from the chains of schooling they were becoming impressively adult in their approach to the real challenges of life. The authorities must have disturbed and baffled more than they felt able to express, or even acknowledge to themselves.

The Authorities Counterattack

In her many books about the experience of childhood and its effects on the adult psyche, Dr. Alice Miller has noted a sinister and pervasive tendency to react to liberal approaches to children as if they were as dangerous and corrosive of the common good as religious heresies in the Middle Ages. She recalls in one of her books being invited to conduct a television programme about the baneful effects of harshness and corporal punishment on children as they grow up. She noticed that whenever she began to establish her arguments with believable testimony and pointed arguments, the producers of the programme would introduce a diversion of some kind - a song, a piece of music, an irrelevant anecdote - which effectively blunted her message.

They might well have thought of this as nothing more than good, smooth programming, but Dr. Miller became convinced that the foundation of our child-rearing culture, that children must never be allowed to feel, to have ideas of their own or to think of themselves as possessing rights as well as responsibilities, was making itself felt, albeit unconsciously. The programme's producers were unable to allow liberal ideas about children to spread unhindered among the general public.

Whatever the precise nature of the authorities' thinking about Joy Baker's children, I would suggest that this un-acknowledged cultural suspicion of anything which might lead to more freedom for children induced them to throw all their resources into pursuing the case. It ought never to have been launched in the first place.

because the evidence of Joy's success in educating her children was as clear as any court could demand. Her children were happy, polite, inquisitive and eminently well prepared for 'real life', whatever that might prove to be.

The tragedy of the situation came not from the authorities' inability to recognise this, but rather from their conviction that children could not be 'educated' without going through the school process, whatever measure of maturity and good learning they might be able to display. The authorities saw schooling as an inescapable social duty like National Service, whose essence was as much its inescapability as any social grace or good learning it enable a young person to acquire.

Chapter seven

Back in Court

On November 6th 1957 Joy went once again to Dereham Magistrates Court to answer new charges of failing to send her children to school. She had hoped that the previous appearance which she had made, at the end of which the decision had seemed to be favourable to her, would see the end of the whole business. She may well have remembered the commonly understood principle of English law that once a person has been acquitted of a charge he or she cannot be brought back and retried for it. Unfortunately, she was not allowed to profit by it because, it seems, there are some things which are so important that mere legal principle cannot be allowed to hinder their prosecution.

She had a sheaf of papers containing her case. They were substantially the same as those she had brought to the previous hearing. She was ready to explain at length how she was bringing up her children even though she had already done so in the presence of the same local authority.

The process began, as it had to, with yet another statement from the authorities. They laid out before the magistrates the whole history of their attempts to bring the Baker children into the classroom, and their mother's endlessly reasoned refusals to comply. Joy took them through their actions and showed that they had, in fact, been given a full and detailed exposition of the education she was giving her children. They had not accepted it, but were completely unable to say why, or indeed why they believed that their schools offered a better education than hers. She hammered home the point she had made several times before, that the authority, in their attendance orders, constantly asserted that such-and-such a school was 'considered suitable' for Joy's children, but could never say exactly how they assessed that suitability.

We should, perhaps, pause for a moment, to think about the implications of that position. If we were constructing an education system for the 21st Century, where there had never been such a thing before, I suspect we would create something very different from the school-based methods we use at the moment. We have become used to the idea that you cannot usefully meet the needs of whole classes of people with a single, one-size-fits-all repertoire of treatments and procedures. We tend nowadays to assume that before any 'professional' who works on or for us will devote some time, at least, to finding out what our needs happen to be.

In previous generations patients were expected to accept without question a doctor's opinion about what was wrong with them. The doctor could not be wrong, and even if he was, the patient was in no position to complain, having no training or knowledge of anatomy on which to base a contrary opinion. In more recent times, however, it has come to be accepted that all patients knows one thing about themselves better than any doctor: how they feel in themselves. That feeling is now recognised as a vitally important component of a comprehensive diagnosis. In these days of holistic medicine, of people-centred social work and the growing recognition that everything we do for others has to be a response to their uniqueness and individuality, we would, I believe, be forced to create a system of education which shared that perception of its purposes. We should have no choice but to be thoroughly learner-centred.

The hearing continued, and Joy ended her examination of Mr. Earl with an enquiry about the delay in bringing the action in which they were now involved. Mr. Earl asserted that Joy had given him the impression that she might send young David to school. He claimed that he had held back from issuing new attendance orders in order to give her the opportunity to choose a school for him. Joy replied that she had certainly given the matter some thought, but had decided against sending her boy into a classroom for his education.

She went on to reiterate that she did not believe in school education, since it was wrong to separate upbringing and instruction, and education should be the combining of both in the secure and natural surroundings of the child's home. That point of view had been upheld by the Quarter Sessions Appeals Committee in Norwich some two years previously.

Joy continued with her testimony, repeating much that had already been said, and standing foursquare behind her radical assertion that 'compulsory education is a contradiction in terms':

> "At school you can sit children in rows at desks and tell them things and you may instruct a proportion of them more or less adequately in a number of quite useless subjects, but this is not education... The time at which education starts is when we are born - and there is no 'leaving age'. We are all still being educated - we absorb knowledge and understanding as we live. So do children - except during the unfortunate period of their lives when they are shut up in school."

The court was not standing up well to the range of Joy's explanation. She was asked if she had much more to say, and when she said that she had, the hearing was adjourned until the next day. It was clear that officialdom was not comfortable with an extensive and detailed exposition of education, particularly when it was being offered by a 'non-professional' who was clearly dedicated to declaring their expertise to be integrally worthless. To them, education was a simple business. You put children into classrooms, dictated to them how they were to see their surroundings and learn about them, and at the end of the process you pitched them out into the world of adulthood supposedly equipped to make sense of their lives.

If any of them failed - and many did - it was their fault. Joy seemed to them to be complicating the whole issue for no good reason. For her, every human experience was potentially educative. She seemed to be determined to treat even the most apparently trivial aspects of life as important and a positive part of her children's education. What they would have stigmatised out of hand as 'time-wasting', had the same status in her eyes as really important things like Pythagoras' theorem or the principal exports of Brazil.

She saw domestic chores, photography, farm-stock management and cooking, as equal to anything a teacher might have spent years learning about. She was denying to a whole profession the prestige which they had spent two-thirds of a century struggling to acquire, by declaring that their accumulated cleverness, their years of study and concentration on rigour and clarity of thought, together with their mainly theoretical consideration of children's ways of thinking, made them largely unable even to perceive their children's real needs, still less meet them. Her stand was more than an attempt to do things differently: it was an insult to an entire community of thought and practice. Her treatment of her children aroused suspicion not only because it was unconventional, but also because it had at its heart a dangerous and subversive idea - that children need a lot less direction and supervision, and a great deal more freedom than our culture has ever extended to them.

The authorities, whether they realised it or not, were defending not simply the letter of the law but also the pyramid of power in which adults stand forever over children, manipulating them, brushing aside their aspirations and affirming their own natural ascendancy for as long as their superiority in physical strength and presence allows them to. That might explain the authority's persistent refusal to discuss with Joy her philosophy of education. Perhaps they feared that if they entered into a dialogue with her they might find themselves having to concede that her ideas had more depth and internal consistency than theirs. This would have thrown into question the whole view of children and their needs to which the school system gave expression.

At this point in the hearing Joy described each of her children. David, aged 12, was the all-rounder in the team. He was strong, skilful and active. He was mainly interested in farming, and spent much of his time learning the work of the surrounding farms. At the same time he was attracted by the Law, and was thinking about becoming a barrister. He had also taken up photography, and had shown outstanding natural ability in it after only three months, winning a prize offered by the *Parents* magazine.

Robin, 11, was entirely different:

> "*lacking David's power of concentration and width of interest; but he has a manual neatness that David lacks. He has unusual domestic ability and is an excellent cook. He is a keen gardener, as well as sharing David's interest in farming, especially where the care of animals is concerned. His main educational needs at present are not academic, but (rather) the development of his individual tastes and sense of responsibility - the reverse of which would be encouraged in school*"

Next came Felicity, aged 9. She was a happy child, Joy asserted, and *"a woman in miniature"*. She was ready, Joy said, to learn 'scholastic subjects' as long as they were associated with practical things. She could ride a horse bareback at a gallop, though she had never had riding lessons. She could care for a baby completely single-handed, dressing, feeding, bathing and changing nappies *"with a great deal more skill than I, who only had a school education, could bring to my first child"*. She had started to learn to read from necessity, since she had had to take charge of her year-old brother when Joy went into hospital to have her last baby, and needed to read the names of the baby foods which she had to feed to her brother.

She had been able to take charge of both babies during Joy's absences from the home on legal business. She was learning to cook, and could clean a room more efficiently than her mother, and she still believed in fairies. Joy could not think of any reason why *"any sane person should want to turn her into that awkward, giggling, school-uniformed monstrosity, a schoolgirl"*.

The next child, Wendy, was eight-years-old. Joy's description of her was long and detailed.

"Wendy...is the problem of my family. She is immature, without being backward in intelligence in any degree. She is unteachable, but, given the right circumstances, quick to learn. She is aggressive, and yet nervous to the point of paralysing shyness when faced with anything of which she is afraid, and she is afraid of anything with which she is not allowed and helped to become acquainted

gradually and in her own time. She is slow in learning to read, but she can make up stories of incredible length and imaginative quality. She is impatient of dry facts, but has a love of poetry even when she cannot comprehend the meaning of the words... There is nothing any intelligent parent can do for such a child other than to offer what instruction the mind is ready for, and leave the rest to the progress of the child's natural development."

Joy went on to mention how the school inspector's visit had scared Wendy because, at the time, two years before, she had found learning the alphabet simply impossible. Joy said that her job was not to force her to overcome her 'problem', but simply to tell her that it did not matter, whereupon she had relaxed, returned to normal, and a year later she learnt the alphabet in less than an hour. She had gone on to to learn to read, slowly and laboriously, but with none of the anguish so many young people associate with literacy.

Joy's testimony went on, setting out her conviction that manners, sociability and interest were ultimately far more worth cultivating than endless tracts of book-knowledge, unrelated to anything her children might want to know about for their own private reasons. At the end of a long day she turned to the Bench and gave them her final address:

"You have heard my statements and the evidence for the prosecution. I submit that these proceedings are not a matter of law, but a matter of opinion as to what suitable education should consist of. No amount of

argument can decide which view is right - mine or the Education Authority's. But I am not seeking to force my view on anyone else's children - it is the Education Authority who seek to force theirs on mine. Is not the whole point of this case whether under the present Act the individual parents have, or have not, the right to decide on the most suitable education for their own child?

"*I submit that the Act allows some freedom to the individual, and that the education I am giving to my children is efficient, full-time education suitable to their ages, abilities and aptitudes within the meaning of the Act; and I claim the right to hold, and act on, my own views in this matter of the education of my own children.*

"*I therefore ask you to dismiss these summonses and allow me to bring up and educate my children in peace.*"

That ought, in all conscience, to have been the end of it, but the magistrates were still not satisfied. They adjourned the matter for a week so that the older children could be brought to the court and questioned by them.

David went in first, having chosen to go and see the magistrates alone. He returned after half an hour with written work to do, including a grocery bill to add up. Then Joy went into the room with the other children. Felicity dissolved into tears when told to pass baby Martin to her mother. Her care for him was the only thing she understood in that intimidating room, facing five unknown people one of whom asked her what she wanted to do when she grew up. She was far too shy to share her real ambition, which at that time was to marry a man who had plenty of horses, and to have lots of babies.

David knocked at the door and came in, asking the magistrates to tell him what a particular number on the written paper they had given him might be. He returned to the anteroom where he had been put to do his work.

One of the magistrates then produced a book with coloured pictures of wild animals, remarking to the others, *"I pinched this from the library"*. Felicity was astonished to learn that magistrates pinched things, but she named all the animals he showed her without hesitation.

Finally, a magistrate who had not yet spoken barked at Felicity. *"What day is it?"* She was surprised that he did not know, especially since the court always sat on a Friday, but supplied the information he asked for politely.

When the 'examination' was over Joy asked David what the magistrates had asked him. She wanted to know whether they had asked him about the things which particularly interested him - farming, Antarctica, photography. They had not shown any interest in farming (on which David was already something of an expert), nor the Antarctic. David's photographs had aroused only limited interest. They had asked him who the captain of England's cricket team was, which he had answered accurately, and which monarch's heads were to be seen on some coins

- he knew them too - followed by a lot of questions about sport. He must have answered them more or less accurately because a lady magistrate kept saying *"Jolly good".*

He had written his name and address and read part of an article from the Reader's Digest. One of his interrogators had even asked him a questions about camels, which David had answered correctly but had been told he was wrong. The question was about what camels stored in their humps. David had said it was fat (as indeed it is), but the magistrate had insisted that it was water. David persuaded him to consult a book on the subject, and the magistrate's error had been revealed.

Inevitably, the magistrates found against Joy, and fined her two pounds, ten shillings for each child. She gave them notice of appeal, and left, amidst flashing cameras and clamouring reporters, who were intent on writing up the journalistically significant aspect of the day's events: *'Boy Puts J.P.s Right About Camels'* and *'Home-School David Stumps J.P.s Over The Camel's Hump.'*

Chapter eight

Up the Down Escalator

The most astonishing aspect of this series of trials is not that they took place over a prodigious length of time, or even that they were defended by a person who had never before set foot in a court of law. It is rather that the case she presented was admirable in its clarity and precision, and it did not change or vary over the months, and even years, during which she presented it. She had none of the characteristics of a criminal, and her appearances in magistrates' courts were entirely uncoloured by the usual atmosphere of resentment and frustration which accompany legal proceedings. She was in a unique position, wholeheartedly committed to doing what the law demands, but unable to convince the custodians of that law that her actions amounted to compliance with it.

This ought, of course, to have prompted a thorough re-evaluation of the part the law plays in promoting the social health of our nation. It has always seemed to me that a crude but fairly safe test of the justice of a law is the type of people who disobey it. If your law results in priests, rabbis, Quakers, nuns and other thoroughly decent people being dragged before the courts you ought, in all conscience, to ask why, and think urgently about what needs to be changed.

Nothing of the sort happened in Joy's case, and her story is a chronicle of repeated trials, appeals, threats and refusals by authority to behave as if it had heard and digested her ideas about education. She went to the Quarter Sessions and appeared before Lord Evershed, the Master of the Rolls, who heard her presentation of her case and accorded it the same degree of attention as the magistrates and earlier judges.

He was mainly concerned about the qualifications which he imagined young people could only obtain from schooling. (We should, perhaps, reflect that this was happening at a time when only grammar school children were routinely entered for public examinations, and other secondary schools were often discouraged from allowing their pupils access to G.C.E. courses.) He did ask Joy whether any of her children had ever been in trouble with the police, and commented favourably on the fact that they had not, but was unable to free himself from the belief that schooling was the only possible mechanism by which a child might be brought from the imagined isolation of his home into the 'wider world', with all its stresses and demands.

Of course, he refused the appeal. Joy told yet another throng of reporters that she would not be sending her children to school.

David won a photographic competition set by *Parents* magazine. He had entered a photograph of Felicity with two young racehorses. The prize was £30 - probably close to £500 in present-day values - with which he bought the new clothes, a tweed jacket, grey flannel trousers and Burberry which he wore for the family's next appearance in court. This took place at Dereham Magistrates' Court, the arena in which Joy had already made two appearances, both of them long-drawn-out and frustrating because neither side was actually communicating with the other.

The dialogue between the determined amateur and the ranks of the professionally deaf went on as Joy had come to expect it would. The authorities presented their simple case - Joy had been ordered to send her children to school and had not done so. Joy rose and began the wearisome task of telling the magistrates yet again what she was doing and why:

> "I think it is already clear that I am not trying to prove that I am teaching my children as they would be taught at school. I am educating my children at home because I do not believe in school education. The Education Act requires that children shall receive efficient full-time education, but in enforcing this regulation the education Authorities appear to assume that the only meaning of the term 'education' is that type of education provided in State schools. There are, of course, many types of education, and only by varying widely educational methods can any education be suitable to the child's ability and aptitude, as the Act also requires. It is in fact a contradiction in terms to require that education be suited to the child's ability and aptitude, and at the same time that it must follow only one rigid pattern as decreed by a Government department."

Joy had exposed in a few well-chosen words the fault which lay at the heart of all government talk about education: with power is assumed to come the right which Lewis Carrol's character Humpty Dumpty claimed for himself - *"A word means exactly what I wish it to mean, neither more nor less"*. Our governors have become expert at verbal plasticity, establishing structures which can be conveniently staffed and paid for, and then surrounding them with a package of words which often express not the reality of those systems, but rather the idealism by means of which their framers convinced the masses to vote for them.

Joy presented the rest of her case as it had been set out in court many times before. She described her children, and the different approaches which they needed, and she challenged many of the assumptions schools make about the 'importance' of their subjects. When she had finished, Mr. Brighton from the authority asked her two simple questions: *"Mrs. Baker, have you any intention of complying with these school attendance orders?"* *"None whatsoever"*, she replied, firmly.

"Do you realise", said Mr. Brighton, with a sigh, *"that there is a century of experience behind the Education Act?"*. Joy replied: *"The fundamental right of a parent to educate her children is even older."*

Mr. Brighton sat down, and Joy called her son David to the witness-box, where she drew out of him his interest in photography and the fact that he had won a competition, and his interest in farming, as a result of which he could milk cows by hand or machine, drive a tractor, work a combine harvester, plough and drill corn. Then Joy asked him to read to the court, and suggested that the magistrates choose something for him to read. The clerk of the court, Mr. Allwood, gave him the *Parents* magazine and got him to read a section from the editorial, which he did clearly and without hesitation.

Joy drew all the reasonable conclusions from her testimony and David's appearance in the witness-box, and concluded her testimony. The chairman, a military man called Brigadier Hervey, told Joy that the magistrates were considering hauling her children before a Juvenile Court, with a view to taking them into care. Joy replied, heatedly, that she would not abandon her duty because of threats. Brigadier Hervey then fined her £1 on each summons, and she gave notice of her intention, yet again, to appeal.

The appeal was heard at the Shire Hall in Norwich before Judge Carey Evans. Michael Havers, who was later to achieve a measure of prominence in public life, appeared for the authority. He addressed himself to his task with vigour, reminding Joy, as if she needed reminding, that her children were in danger of having to appear in a Juvenile Court, after which dire penalties might well follow. He painted a picture of Joy as selfish and obstinate, and pointed out that she was not 'qualified in any way to teach'.

At this point a note arrived from Joy's lawyer, Mr. Hipwell, who had not been able to come to Court. It simply said *"Press for autrefois convict"*. Joy did not know what this arcane piece of legal French meant, but an inspired guess enabled her to tell the judge that she had already been convicted and fined on two occasions for having failed to comply with four attendance orders. No date had been given for the offences, but in each case the orders were given the same date, 19th July 1957. It therefore appeared that she had been convicted and fined twice for the same offence.

Judge Evans did not agree, and the appeal went on, in clear contravention of a principle of law which until very recently was unchallengeable - a person may not be punished for the same offence twice. It was becoming clear that education law was a reservation fenced off from the main stream of both common and statute law, where authority could make up the rules as it went along, and violate both justice and good common sense at will.

The case continued along well-worn lines. Joy presented her older children, and used them to demonstrate the indubitably high standard of education they were receiving. Joy made all the usual points, and ended her speech with a statement which anyone with an ounce of common sense would endorse without a moment's hesitation:

> *"Many people would believe it impossible in this country that my children could be brought before a Juvenile Court and taken away from me on the sole grounds that I do not send*

them to school. They cannot be said to be in need of care on this or any other grounds; they are not neglected or damaged in any way."

She asked the judge to declare that her provision for her children was adequate. With ill-concealed impatience he refused. Joy appealed, asking for a case to be stated on the grounds that the justices were wrong in law in their determination of her case.

The appeal was innocent of any attempt to respond to Joy's testimony about her children's upbringing. The case stated was expensive, and Joy could not get legal aid, but she was able to pass all the documents to London, and at last, on 5th February, 1960, she appeared before the Lord Chief Justice in the Divisional Court.

It would be encouraging to discover that the professional lawyers had a clearer sight of the issues at stake in this case than the relative amateurs who sat on the benches of the magistrates' courts. Unfortunately, Lord Parker, the Lord Chief Justice found against her in much the same terms as everyone else who had heard her testimony, and Mr. Justice Ashworth and Mr. Justice Davies agreed. Only one concession was allowed her. David, who was now within hailing distance of school leaving age, (then 15) need not go to school. The Lord Chief Justice had said so.

102 Chris Shute

Chapter nine

The Last Stretch

The process had taken ten years. The authority had fired its salvoes of legal power and Joy had managed to parry them, without diminishing her adversary's enthusiasm for the battle. To us, viewing the affair from nearly 50 years in the future, it might seem that the bureaucracy of that time was in urgent need of cost-benefit analysis. Clearly their priorities were compliance and submission, rather than any conceivable advantage which might accrue to the Baker children.

The next step in the children's tortuous path to freedom was an application for them to be made wards of court, in order that they might be compelled to go to school, whatever they or their mother might have thought about it. This measure, which was sometimes used in cases where underage children were in genuine moral or physical danger, would not necessarily have taken them from their parents' home, but it would certainly have removed Joy from having any effective influence over their education.

Fortunately, by the time the application was heard in the Chancery Court in London, Joy's barrister, Mr. W. A. Bagnall, Q.C., had managed to draw the proceedings out so that the best part of another year had slipped by, and his presentation of the case was sufficiently abundant in technicalities that he was able to persuade Mr. Justice Pennycuick that he had no jurisdiction in the matter. The application for the children's wardship was rejected.

The authority's indomitable Mr. Sparrow appealed, and on May 30th 1961 Lord Justices Ormerod, Upjohn and Pearson heard his latest attempt to bring the Baker children into the school system.

His line of attack incorporated a new element. Joy had mentioned in her testimony that her children took part in the usual round of domestic chores. Mr. Sparrow attempted to parlay this into a form of domestic slavery, asserting that the children were mainly being kept at home as unpaid cleaners and cooks. This carried little weight with the judges, but furnished the press with lurid headlines along the lines of *'Children Used As Servants.'*

The final phase of this bizarre journey through the courts is interesting more for the light it sheds on the law's delays than for anything which might be learned from it about education. Joy's eldest son had been born in 1945: it was not until 1961 that light appeared at the end of the tunnel, and even then it seemed to be attached to an oncoming locomotive.

Joy was arraigned before the magistrates yet again, and her extensive presentation of the reality of her children's education was received with the same utter indifference as it had received on every other occasion. This time, however, the magistrates sentenced Joy to two months in prison. A policeman appeared as she left the court and served on her two summonses for Felicity and Wendy to appear before the Juvenile Court. Joy accorded them the same respect as she had given to the attendance orders she had been given at the beginning of her ordeal. She tore them up and gave them to her counsel, Mr. Hipwell, as she left the court, having been given bail until the hearing of her appeal.

The idea of putting children before the Juvenile Court to answer for decisions taken by their parents would seem, I suppose, to reflect a more brisk and uncomplicated approach to childhood than we would expect now. Unfortunately, children who do not go to school are still put under a degree of pressure by certain local authorities even today.

There is a growing recognition that some parents wish to educate their children at home, and they are sometimes allowed to do so, but I have met enough inspectors during visits to home-educating families to have formed the impression that in their heart of hearts they are still looking for lessons, written work, long hours spent in something like a classroom, and evidence of an intention to put youngsters through the same examinations as schooled children. Education is still, or so it seems to the professionals, a process which can only validly be done to children validly by trained teachers.

Joy had only a month to prepare herself for the possibility of going to prison. She tried to make arrangements for the care of her children, but, as one can readily imagine, the strain was making her ill.

Mr. Hipwell advised her that she should appeal only against the sentence, not against the conviction, advice which was confirmed by the barrister who would appear for her in the appeal, Mr. Geoffrey Leach. It seemed that if she appealed against the conviction she would almost certainly go to prison. Joy rejected that advice without any hesitation. She was not prepared to turn her back on the position which she had been defending for more than ten years. To accept that she was guilty of depriving her children of education and to ask for the mercy of the court was too humiliating for her to contemplate.

On November 15th Joy made her way to the Shirehall in Norwich. She was familiar with the setting, but this time there was an ominous difference: she was taken in charge by a woman prison officer from Holloway prison. Together they went into the court through a door on which was painted 'GOALER'S ENTRANCE'. Joy pointed to it and asked her escort *"Who painted that?"* The officer replied, with a grin, *"Someone who had been to school!"*

She entered the dock, and the prison officer took away her handbag. She was a prisoner. This mother, who had brought her children up with consummate skill and dedication had to accept the shame and humiliation which was inseparable from the status of convicted prisoner.

The magistrates entered, led by their chairman, Mr. Roger North, and took their places. Mr. Ives, from the authority, said all the usual things: it was the authority's task to see that every child in their area received an efficient, full-time education suitable to its age and aptitude, and the authority had a duty to take proceedings against any parent who failed to conform to this statute. Mrs. Baker had failed to satisfy the authority in that regard.

Mr. Earl gave his usual testimony about his attempts to 'inspect' Joy's educational efforts. Mr. Leach asked him about Joy's general care for her children:

"There is no suggestion that Mrs. Baker is not doing her best for these children?"

"She provides food, clothing and shelter", he replied.

"She is a good mother?" pressed Mr. Leach.

"I prefer not to comment", was Mr. Earl's rejoinder.

When Mr. Earl had finished his evidence, Joy went into the witness box. Mr. Leach asked her about her work with the children, and she replied:

"None of my children", she said, *"have ever been to school. They have all learned reading, writing and basic arithmetic. They have learned history and geography from the school programmes on the radio, and from books. In their everyday life they have learned natural*

history, riding, cookery and photography, and the girls have learned household management and child care. They have all been taught to speak well and behave well."

"Education is a training for life", she went on. "It is too wide a subject to be confined within the four walls of a classroom. My children do not sit at desks to study set lessons at set times. They are taught a subject when they show interest in it. When they are interested they ask questions, and are told what they want to know."

She also pointed out that everyone who had met the children agreed that they were well spoken, well-mannered and well-behaved.

She described her children in detail. Felicity was at a ballet school in Norwich where she was showing considerable talent. She was also a good photographer and horse-rider. David was a stockman, and had already taken charge of a herd of ten pedigree Jersey cows while his employer was away on holiday. He was now working with a show herd of 70 cows of the same breed on a 3000-acre farm in Cambridgeshire. His employers spoke highly of him. Robin, who was now 15, was working as a plasterer - a highly skilled trade. His employers spoke well of him, also. It was clear that Lord Evershed's fears about her children being unable to make their way in the world of adult work were misplaced.

The giving of evidence revealed nothing which had not been said with equal eloquence before.

The Last Stretch

All that remained was for Mr. Leach to give his final speech for the defence.

The principal requirement of the Education Act, he told the court, was that children should receive an education which would foster the spiritual, moral, mental and physical development. On three of these - spiritual, moral and physical - there was no dispute.

On the fourth - mental development - can this be achieved only by sitting behind wooden desks in a secondary modern school? These schools do not even give a certificate of education comparable with other schools.

> *"This lady is not a crank,"* he said, *"but someone who holds very strong views about the education of her children."*

He asked the court to say that Joy had given and was giving her children education which would meet the requirements of the Education Act.

The Justices retired, and Joy settled down to wait. She asked if there were any appeals which could be made, and Mr. Leach said that there were, but her legal aid certificate did not cover them. He began to tutor her in the precise procedures she would have to know about to make the appeal herself, but he could see that she was too preoccupied to take it in. He agreed to ask for the appeal himself and worry about the fees later.

The Justices returned.

Mr North began giving their verdict:

> "What we have to decide," he said, "is whether the education these children are getting complies with the Education Act of 1944. We cannot see that it doesn't..."

Joy began to realise what Mr. North was saying.

> "Mrs Baker has told us a great deal about her views on education, and we cannot see that what she has described fails to satisfy the rather wide terms of the Education Act. The appeal therefore succeeds."

It would be pleasant to record that the authority recognised Joy's victory and allowed her to turn her full attention back to the education of her children. She certainly expected to be left alone. Unfortunately, local authorities do not like to lose their engagements with ordinary people, and it was not long before Joy was notified of an appeal by the authority against the Justices decision.

The appeal to the Divisional Court was delayed by another year, but finally Joy took her place in front of the Lord Chief Justice. Once again the authority's representative presented what must have become, by then, one of the most frequently explained prosecution cases in the history of English law. On the other side, the Justices had given Mr. Leach a statement of their intentions which he placed before the Court:

> "We are of the opinion" "that the Appellant had proved that the education given to the said children complied with efficient, full-time education as meant by the Education Act 1944 and that the Appellant had not failed to cause

the said children to receive efficient full-time education suitable to their age and aptitude otherwise than by regular attendance at school and accordingly allowed the Appeals."

Counsel for the authority, Mr. Paul Wrightson, argued that the Justices' decision was 'perverse', but he spoke without much conviction, and with very little in the way of serious evidence. He read out extracts from Joy's evidence, given during her earlier appearances in court. *"You will see, my Lord"*, he said, almost plaintively, *"that in all these cases Mrs. Baker has said exactly the same thing."* Why this should have been taken as an adverse criticism of her position is hard to see, and it carried no weight with Lord Parker, who listened to Mr. Wrightson for another hour, before conferring with Mr. Justice Widgery and Mr. Justice Winn, and delivering his decision. Lord Parker told Mr. Leach, Joy's counsel, that it would not be necessary for him to present her case:

"The appeal committee was satisfied that Mrs. Baker is giving the children efficient full-time education. A very strong case must be shown for this court to say that no reasonable bench of magistrates could come to that conclusion",

Lord Parker also commented on Joy's approach to children's learning.

"All children", he said, *"start learning by asking questions. It is a recognised method of education."*

The Authority's appeal was dismissed. The battle was over, and Joy had won.

Chapter ten

Conclusion

All this happened more than fifty years ago. The world of education has changed, at least superficially, and the right of parents to educate their children out of school has been recognised by most local authorities. If she were trying to do now what she did in the forties and fifties of the last century Joy Baker would find relatively few obstacles placed in her path by educational professionals. They would still want to come and 'inspect' what she was doing, but if my experience of such encounters is anything to go by she would probably find the visitor more or less ready to give formal consent to the sort of programme she outlined to the courts. The battle she fought alone has been won by such groups as Education Otherwise and Home Education Advisory Service, and increasing numbers of children are growing up without necessarily having to spend eleven years sitting in classrooms and listening to teachers talking.

Yet at a deeper level Joy's campaign is still going on. The case she made out against the institution of school is still not recognised by anyone whose voice is listened to and acted on in the world of education. The idea of a parent taking responsibility for imparting knowledge to her children is still seen by most English people as an aberration, albeit not as serious a departure from normality as it seemed to be just after World

War 2. The network of knowledge control and authoritarianism which is a school, is still seen by ordinary folk, often in a culpably vague way, as essential for the proper development of children.

By writing this book I hope to ask why and to propose a radical answer to that question.

One thing emerges from the story of Joy Baker with irresistible force: she loved and respected her children. Many teachers and administrators would probably say the same about the children they have to deal with, but the striking aspect of Joy's definition of 'respect', which differentiates it from any which might have been held by the authorities who persecuted her, was that it was based on meeting the children's needs as they presented themselves. She did not think, as the generality of educators still do, that children 'need' to be taught certain things at certain ages, whether they express interest in them or not. She refused to share the culturally ingrained picture of childhood which holds that it is a time when people are essentially empty, undefined, incapable of serious thought or of choosing sensible, altruistic courses of action unless firmly compelled to do so. Consequently, the authorities could not persuade her that they could educate her children without either knowing them or finding out what they might be disposed to learn.

Joy's ideas about education were clearly dangerous to those authorities for a number of different possible reasons. At the most superficial level they represented a threat to the universality of the law. Parliament, in which the

Conclusion and Postscript

Nation had vested its ultimate power to direct its individual members because it was imagined to embody the best wisdom which could be procured, had provided schools and made a rule that all children should go to them. This was for the best, or so it appeared, because schools provided a way in which our culture could be imparted, more or less conveniently, to the rising generation. This was clearly held to be good and necessary. If any individual decided not to co-operate they were openly rebelling against the power of the state and by implication putting in peril the stability of a whole people.

A deeper analysis of Joy's action might have revealed that she was challenging an integral culture, widely spread throughout Europe and the Anglo-Saxon world, which holds that children are, among many other things, a different kind of human being from adults, dangerous, skittish and unable to make good decisions for themselves. They have, of course, the potential to become, by a miracle not unlike that which transforms a nondescript pupa into a beautiful butterfly, a fully competent adult, but until that time comes they need to be supervised, restrained, compelled to act against their inclinations and never allowed to think that they know more about their own needs than the adults who surround them. Driven by the pervasive Christian idea that all children bear the taint of Original Sin, our culture insists that children need to have their every 'wrongdoing' pointed out to them and duly punished. The nature and severity of the punishment will depend on the enthusiasm of parents and teachers for its infliction, but the possibility of a childhood without rebukes and sanctions is not a serious proposition. Our love for our children allows us to like them, in the intervals between their misbehaviours, but woe betide the parent who suggests that a child can live without being told off at regular intervals. He or she will usually be characterised as weak, irrational and even part of a liberal conspiracy against 'healthy, Old English values'.

Joy Baker did not share that traditional view of childhood. She saw her children's earliest years as a precious time during which each new member of her family discovered the unique, unrepeatable structure of interests and emotions of which their personality was made. She saw it as her special responsibility, as their parent, to begin imparting to them her culture and her values. She did not see the educator's task as one of handing on knowledge and forcing young people to memorise it. That would be, in her eyes, little better than the mass medication of patients whether they were ill or not. She wanted her children to discover for themselves how they could live in what the poet Robert Graves described as:

> ....*This endless, only world*
> *In which we say we live.*

Inevitably this involved allowing them to decide for themselves when, and whether, they learned the things which parents and teachers have decided are 'important'.

This is the point at which all serious educational thinking has to decide which of two contrary paths it will pursue. Either we - society, adults, authority, government - believe that young human beings are broadly similar, needing to undergo the same interventions in their lives at the same ages and stages in their development, or we recognise that each person is unique. If we hold the latter position we cannot honestly endorse the present structure of education. It represents an inhumane, stultifying process, which presents knowledge to the young learner as a series of things which they have to learn in order to be safe and to please the grownups, whether or not those things happen to engage their private interest. Frequently schoolteachers argue that their pupils have to learn boring facts and unstimulating disciplines for no better reason than that when they grow up 'they will have to do things they don't want to do'. That this is not recognised as a shameful thing to say in an educational context causes me to wonder 'why not?' Certainly it goes some way towards justifying the comment attributed to a Conservative writer, that 'taxi drivers know as much about education as teachers'. Or as little, for that matter.

Joy Baker repudiated that authoritarian view of education in root and branch. She was challenged at one point to show that she was 'qualified' to educate her children. The prevailing view at the time - it still persists - was that only certain people could be educators. They had to have been 'trained' and by virtue of their training they were supposed to know things about children which ordinary people could not be expected to understand. Joy, however, felt that as her children's mother she was infinitely better placed than any expert could ever be to meet their needs. By adopting that stance she was, as we have seen, rejecting not just the local provision of schools, but also the basis of school-based education. She would not accept that 'education' was only happening when some more or less learned person was standing in front of thirty-odd children making them memorise facts and do exercises designed to make them as literate and numerate as they were needed to be.

The shape which schooling possessed then, the grim, regimented daily dragging of children through lessons which interested them, if at all, only sporadically, has survived a century, and any attempts to reform it. This is, I would suggest, for four reasons. It is relatively cheap, compared with individual or small-group tuition, it provides dependable employment for teachers, it meets parents' need to have their children looked after during the working day, and it enables society to claim that it has given equal chances to all its young adults. That does not even remotely correspond to what research has shown children really need. It is a soulless process which many children instinctively react against, and the best way our modern society has found to deal with such disaffection is to punish parents for not making their children go to school.

Joy Baker saw through this regrettable mishandling of childhood. She realised that her children would gain knowledge from many different sources, by experience as much as by passive listening or reading books. She also realised that teaching often hinders learning. Her own experience of schooling had left her with memories of being confused, overwhelmed by new knowledge which she could not assimilate in time. She knew by instinct as much as by reflection that for her family at least schooling would be stultifying and restricting experience.

What, then, was the message she was trying to convey to the wider world? Certainly not that the government should close its schools with all haste. She never gave any thought to the reconstruction of the education system. Her concern was bounded entirely by the interests of her family. As far as she was concerned she was doing no more than her status as a parent imposed on her. She was protecting her children from a danger whose reality she could not deny. The fact that the danger she perceived came from an institution as venerable, and compulsory as school attendance did not change her clear-eyed determination to keep her children out of its clutches. I suspect that what she demonstrated was not so much courage, though she needed a full measure of that, as a feeling not entirely unlike that felt, perhaps, by the pilot of a crashing aircraft: jumping out and deploying his parachute would be the last thing he intended or wished to do, but in the circumstances it could not be avoided. Beyond that, Joy had no message for the Establishment.

Yet everything she said to the various courts and tribunals before which she appeared, made up a dynamic, uncompromising critique of the whole system by which British children were educated.

First, she insisted on the absolute uniqueness of every child. This could not be avoided or compromised. It seemed absurd to her that decisions about her children's education could be arrived at by people who had never met them, knew nothing about them as individuals, and had already decided and codified what they were going to be taught. Many parents would agree with her in general terms, but they would then allow themselves to be overcome by the apparently unchallengeable argument that to assess every child and educate that child in strict accordance with his or her aptitudes and interests would require a budget beyond the reach even the richest nations. It has become a commonplace of educational debate that schools, in spite of their systemic faults, are as close as we are going to get to the best possible means of educating our children. Joy Baker did not try to conceive an alternative system, but her persistent pressure on the authorities to take notice of her criticisms, together with the undoubted success which she achieved with her own children, causes me, at least, to believe that someone, somewhere in this country, which has so often shown itself intolerant of social injustice, should give active thought to a reform of education from which no professional or financial interest should be protected.

During her visits to schools Joy noticed that many of the children she saw were not having their emotional needs attended to. In one school she observed that the toilets were outside, open to the elements, cold and unwelcoming. She questioned this, but received no acknowledgement that young children might actually need to be able to perform their natural functions in a warm, comfortable and above all, private, place. Their supposedly trained teachers clearly shared the common cultural conviction that being 'soft' on children, taking their feelings to heart and listening to them was both foolish and dangerous, as well as being unreasonably expensive. As it happens, I well remember being sickened by the lavatories at my own primary school. I resented the fact that I often had to endure a full bowel until home time because the thought of using them during break, was unthinkable. Dozens of older, cruder and more mischievous boys would be able to intrude upon possibly the most private activity I could imagine, and I could not bear the thought of that. I realised then, and still hate, the fact that purely because I was only nine or ten-years-old the adults assumed I had no 'real' feelings, no truly 'valid' emotions. Perhaps that is why I grew up with a deep hatred of oppression, particularly racial oppression. Apartheid and slavery seemed to me to be based on an assumption about people which was not far different from what I was living through at school. To racist white people black Africans were not really human, and there was no need to treat them as if they were: indeed it was absurd to do so, as absurd as building palaces to keep cattle in. The same general principle seemed to apply to children, with only real mitigating factor being that sooner or later the oppressed could look forward to growing up and becoming the oppressors in their turn.

In some ways the worst aspect of schooling which Joy discovered during her odyssey through the courts was the simple fact that it was presumed to succeed every time it was applied to any set of children, anywhere. An expensive corps of inspectors was employed to make sure that schools taught what they were supposed to teach, in the manner prescribed by the highest levels of the government's education department. Yet no-one ever investigated the results. No government sponsored survey had ever addressed itself to the question of what the pupils became when they left school, and whether their experience there had made them happier, more effective learners, or whether it had turned them into neurotic philistines. One reason for this is that schooling has become a secular substitute for religion. As such it cannot be thought of as a source of any kind of evil. Just as Christians are happy to point to St. Francis of Assisi or Mother Theresa as examples of religious virtue, conveniently forgetting Torquemada's Inquisition or the Crusades, so proponents of compulsory schooling speak in praise of the growing number of young people who pass out of schools and go to university and college, as if there were not thousands of school leavers who finish their schooling convinced that they are stupid, and who never pick up a serious book again in their entire lives, not to speak of the hordes of youngsters who after eleven years of compulsory religion, do drugs and become burglars or muggers.

Another reason for the belief that schooling 'works' in some sort of universal way is the very professionalism which has grown up around it. In their struggle to be better paid and more highly thought of teachers have turned their work from a relatively simple craft, which could be transmitted to bright children in early teenage (the pupil teachers of the late nineteenth century) into a supposedly complex, intellectually demanding branch of both art and science, for which a degree and three or four years' training are the minimum necessary. Inevitably, teachers come to think that the skills which they took so long to acquire must endow the things they do with value, and their professional opinions with preponderant authority. This in its turn prevents them from seeing when they are, in fact, talking inhumane, mediaeval nonsense. It also allows schools to say all the right things in their prospectuses about 'developing every child's potential', 'emphasising self-discipline', 'preparing the children for adult life' and so on and so forth, because whether they actually succeed or not, their teachers are deemed to be doing a professional job. Therefore, if children do not learn what they need to know it is because they, the children, have deliberately and unreasonably resisted those teachers' efforts. Like doctors whose patients sometimes die, the teachers shrug their shoulders and reflect that they did their honest best against opposition which no-one could have overcome.

Joy Baker had no time for the professionals. She saw in them blinkered people who could not see the real interests of her children because they had already decided what they were and how they would cater for them. She realised that her world-view was so different from theirs that they would see it as 'unprofessional' if they accepted any of her premises. Following George Bernard

Shaw, she saw the professions as conspiracies againt the laity.

Talking about education often involves the comparison of intelligences. Teachers can teach because they are 'intelligent': parents cannot because they 'have not got the intelligence, the knowledge', to be a teacher. This comes about because, from their inception, schools have been about 'subjects'. Knowledge has become detached from the use to which it is put, and has become the stock-in-trade of a class of people called teachers, who hand it out to children who are expected to absorb it because it is there and they are deemed to 'need' it.

Only certain 'subjects' are thought to have value. These are the disciplines which have always formed the core of the British curriculum: maths, English, history, geography, science, modern languages, religion (to inoculate the pupils against sin), physical activity, a certain amount of music, art and craft, and nowadays an introduction to information technology. Anything else, if it is taught at all, will usually be an extramural activity, available only where there is a teacher who happens to know about it.

As a result, for some pupils at least, the things to which they will devote the rest of their lives form no part of their school experience, just like the ballet and the stockmanship which became the centre of the lives of two of Joy's children. This forces many children to waste hundreds, even thousands of hours during their precious childhood doing things which they will never do again, and not learning the basis of their future career.

I well remember watching the development of a family in the education of whose sons I had a small part to play. Neither boy had ever gone to school, and their parents had managed to avoid the attentions of the authority by the simple expedient of never registering them in a school, and beyond the usual initiation into reading and writing they had had no formal teaching, apart from the religion classes which they attended as Jehovah's Witnesses. Yet they are both now, as young men, highly qualified in various branches of information technology and computing.

The younger lad went out with his father and learned from him how to install and maintain burglar alarms, CCTVs, and security gates. When I last met him, in his early twenties, he was a manager of a well-known security equipment company. The most notable thing about him, in my estimation, was that by the time he reached 'school-leaving' age he was already an efficient, skilled and knowledgeable worker, able to earn a good wage and even supervise other workers, as he did when he was seventeen. He managed to do it without offending them, which was a testimony to the social training he had received from his parents. His brother, whom I introduced to computing, went on to find training courses in information technology and computer maintenance and to become a serious businessman, directing his own company and making a good living.

None of this would have happened if these young men had gone to school. The younger lad would never have been allowed to miss his lessons to go out with his father and learn his trade. The elder boy would have had to go through the motions of learning all sorts of things which would have prevented him from beginning to understand computing. their lives would have been very different, and the beginning of their adult lives would have been postponed by several unnecessary years. Like Joy Baker's children, they needed not the attentions of professional teachers, but simply the opportunity to spend time with people who knew how to do useful things which interested them.

As I read *Children in Chancery* I found myself constantly returning to the same question: These authority representatives were not stupid, nor were they vicious. They wanted the best for Joy's children. They had the opportunity to meet them and to see what kind of people they were becoming, without schooling. Why were they so determined to drag them out of an environment which was clearly benefiting them in order to thrust them into another which might not? Obviously it all happened a long time ago, and we can never be absolutely certain, but I tend to the view that at the time the vast majority of British people saw school attendance as the means by which society hardened its young and taught them that they could not have what they wanted, and that they had to adapt to the world and not the other way round. I believe that if we are to remedy the social disaster which turns so many of our young people into criminals, disaffected, workshy philistines and inadequate parents we have to begin by reconfiguring our education system so that it meets the real, felt needs of the children it is supposed to help.

Whenever I propose a system of education based on a large variety of choices, including allowing parents to take full control of their children's upbringing and initiation into life, I notice that the objections which flood in upon me are almost never educational, except in the most general sense. They are far more often economic - 'It would be far too expensive' - or bureaucratic - 'You could never organise it safely and efficiently'. Interestingly, I rarely find that people object to the basic idea of diversity and flexibility in education, and many admit that they would like to extend some, at least, of the freedom which Joy Baker seized for herself to their own situation. The problem as they see it is that the present system is simply too monolithic, and far too convenient for politicians, parents, education authorities and employers to be capable of being changed in any way beyond the purely cosmetic, such as by inventing new names for schools or allowing commercial interests to add the funding of them to their array of good works.

Real root-and-branch reform will need a measure of courage and clarity of thought which few legislators possess. The beginnings of change are already showing themselves very tentatively since the government has, on paper at least, committed itself to exploring 'personalised learning' We can, I think, assume that this does not mean the kind of individualisation which Joy Baker pioneered in her family, but equally clearly it must mean something different from the lockstep march from year one to year eleven, with its imposed learning, manic testing and compulsory curriculum.

The shape of that advance is still difficult to discern. It is clear that governments will continue to base their thinking on the school, as the place where teaching and learning are primarily concentrated. On the other hand, the almost exponential growth of other means of getting or imparting knowledge, the internet, the use of i-pods, the sheer ubiquity of information and the means of passing it from one person to another, have made absurd the proposition that young people can only learn what they need to know by attending school. Also, it has become noticeable that, in spite of the vigour with which right-wing commentators still denounce the softness of judges, policemen, teachers and legislators, liberal initiatives, such as the Human Rights Act and the growing tolerance of non-heterosexual lifestyles, they nevertheless influence the way in which as a nation we respond to the challenges of being human in an advanced, civilised community.

Perhaps as new generations of home-educated children spread their experience more widely and some, at least, see educating their own children at home as natural and normal, the authorities will begin to see their point of view as respectable, and begin to support it, instead of merely 'authorising' it. Even inspectors and administrators are not necessarily illiberal. Their functions impose on them a preoccupation with budgets, 'feasibility' and legal constraints. When the world in which they work begins to change there is a chance their thinking will too.

Good education begins at a human level. It is about feelings and relationships long before it is about Pythagoras or Boyles's Law. Joy Baker knew that, and practised it. Against her were ranged scores of people who, by their conduct and their attitudes, showed that, if they knew it in theory, could not translate that theory into any sort of practice. I would suggest that we must work towards a time when Joy Baker's approach to education becomes the unchallengeable norm, and the attitudes of her opponents are seen as mediaeval, as inappropriate in education as bleeding and leeches would be in modern medicine.

Postscript

In 1963 David was 18, and working with his Jersey herd. Joy described him as *"competent,. reliable, happy in his independence, dreaming of and planning for, the day when he will have a farm of his own."*

Robin, 17, had completed his first term as an apprentice plasterer.˙ He had transferred to a larger firm in Norwich. Unusually he had taken a written exam - the first Baker child to do so - and he was one of the 7 who passed out of his class of 12.

Felicity, at 15, was still training for a career in ballet. She won the Norwich School of Dance and Drama's cup for ballet in July 1963. A well-known teacher said of her 'When she dances she lights up the room.